On Writing BOOKS for CHILDREN

JENNY WAGNER

A LITTLE
ARK
BOOK

ALLEN & UNWIN

Acknowledgements

I would like to thank Lyndall Osborne and the staff at the Nambour Library for their help in researching this book. May no one ever say 'I'm looking for a small red book, but I don't know what it's called' again.

Thanks also to Dr Michael Apthorp of the Classics Department at the University of Queensland, who helped keep my feet out of my mouth.

The quotation from *Rosie's Walk*, by Pat Hutchins, on page 27, is reproduced with the kind permission of Macmillan Publishing Company, New York, and The Bodley Head, London.

First published 1992
A Little Ark Book
Allen & Unwin Pty Ltd
9 Atchison Street, St Leonards
NSW 2065, Australia

National Library of Australia
Cataloguing-in-Publication entry:

Wagner, Jenny.
   On writing books for children.

   Bibliography.
   Includes index.
   ISBN 1 86373 367 1.

   1. Children's stories — Authorship.
   2. Children's stories — Technique.
   I. Title.

806.06833

Cover illustration by Ron Brooks
Designed by Sandra Nobes
Typeset by Bookset
Printed by The Book Printer, Maryborough, Victoria

CONTENTS

Writers who set out to write books on writing are aware of the dangers of what they are doing and arm themselves beforehand. They explain right at the beginning that if they have carelessly mentioned a rule or two it was purely accidental, and readers should take no notice.

I have no intention of breaking with tradition. I'll say right at the outset that there are no rules, and no advice that fits all cases. There are many kinds of children's books, and as many ways to write them as there are writers.

So this book is not a collection of handy hints that will bring you fame and fortune; instead I am giving you a toolbox. I explain what the tools are, what job they do and how they do it; I show you the best ways I know of using them, and how not to hurt your fingers on them. I even suggest some things you might like to make. But I don't claim for one moment that these are the only tools available, or that there is only one way to use them.

The one rule I can state with certainty is: there are no rules; even if there were any, good writers would only break them.

1 GETTING STARTED

The child in you

Writing for children, like selling encyclopaedias or digging ditches (both of which it resembles in some ways) needs no special knowledge and no expensive equipment. All you need to start with are the writer's most basic tools: pencil and paper. Everything else you need is already in you, including the most important thing, an awareness of yourself as a child.

Knowing some real live children is no hindrance — children, being a reminder of your own childhood, can help to awaken the child that still exists in you — but it's not essential. You are already an expert on one child, yourself, and for now that's all you need. The child in you remembers what you need to know, and will guide your writing accordingly.

In spite of this simplicity, many writers have trouble getting started. All that creative freedom is intimidating — there are so many ways to go wrong. Where is the best place to start? What is the best thing to write?

It doesn't matter. The very first things you write will be practice pieces anyway, and a practice piece cannot be wrong. If you don't believe me, here is a five-finger exercise to get you started.

Think back to when you were a child and remember yourself at three different ages. What incidents do you remember that made you feel frightened, happy, angry or sad? What things made you feel bored? Jealous? Choose one incident for each of the three ages.

As you think yourself back into these episodes you'll be surprised at how much you remember: the colour of the afternoon light outside the head-master's door, the smell of your grandmother's furniture, the feel of a dog's fur on your face. All children are observant, and so were you; these memories of your childhood will form much of your raw material.

In fact the most useful material for any writer is that store of memories, but new writers often undervalue it. They are more interested in writing about the things they haven't experienced — living in Japan, belonging to the opposite gender, being a fighter pilot, or living in a world of dragons, princesses, castles, talking dogs and magic rings. The last thing they want is to be fettered by reality.

But there is more to writing good children's books than dreaming up plots and imagining settings out of nothing. By the time the third manuscript starts to yellow in the drawer, most successful writers have realised this. I hope this book will shorten the process for you; there are ways of exploring unknown worlds and at the same time being true to your own experience. But first I have to explain about ideas.

Getting ideas

One question that children's writers are often asked, and find difficult to answer, is 'Where do you get your ideas?' It supposes that a place exists where ideas are to be found: a secret well, perhaps, that only writers know about. Faced with this question a children's writer has two choices: to say something easy but unilluminating like 'My ideas come from everyday life', or to risk frightening the listener by explaining the process in detail. Since you have gone to the trouble of reading this book I'll take the latter course.

It's true that the material in a children's book — the stuff the writing is made of — comes from the writer's life. But more accurately, it comes from two kinds of experience.

At some time, in a quiet, unguarded moment, you have perceived things that interested you and moved you in a way you couldn't explain. I'm not talking about grand visions or inspiration, just ordinary everyday experience: a grey cat on a fence, a quiet street, two people talking, a child absorbed in a secret game. The experiences aren't necessarily visual; perhaps you heard someone singing, or you smelled wet earth, or heard a rooster crowing. The important thing is that the experience had a special significance for you.

These sorts of experience all have one thing in common: they seem to mean more than they say. They convey a special feeling of significance to the person who has them, and that feeling, together with an impulse to discover why a memory is significant, can become so intense that you are obliged to vent it in some way. For people who write, rather than those who sculpt, draw, paint, dance or make music, the need is to contain and make sense of the feeling by clothing it in words. In this way, writing becomes an attempt to discover meaning.

These experiences are the prefiguring ideas that all artists work with, whether they are composers, sculptors, novelists, poets, playwrights or writers of children's books. In fact everyone has them, not just artists: cabinet-makers, geologists, gardeners, nurses, librarians, electricians, taxi-drivers, mothers, fathers and computer programmers have them too. The only difference is that artists take particular notice because they need to work with them.

The second kind of experience is also a memory, but lacks the urgency of the first, and carries no extra meaning. The experience means only what it says. This material is the simple infill of writing; your observations of people and day-to-day living stored away as memories. Your character walks through an empty house, and you draw on your memories of empty houses, of dust and echoing footsteps; a child character eats an ice-cream, and you draw on your memories of hot days when melting ice-cream trickled down your arm. As readers, we accept observations like this as 'true' because we recognise them and share them; for both children and adults, it's an important part of the pleasure of reading. When we read W. H. Auden's 'children, casual as birds', we are delighted, but not because something new has been shown to us. We don't say 'Good heavens! I never thought of it like that before.' We are delighted because we recognise that that is how it is; we have been shown a kind of truth.

People who are not in touch with their childhood experience find this kind of detail hard to remember. How many adults who are not writers remember the irritations of childhood? Socks that migrated down over your heels and made lumps under your feet; jumpers that threatened to amputate your nose when your mother took them off; hair that tangled itself into a bird's nest overnight; trickles of cold water running down your arms when you reached up to wash your hands.

Inexperienced writers often believe that this kind of detail can be researched; if you need to set a story in Iceland, they say, all you have to do is talk to someone who has been there, or read a book about it. But it's a poor substitute for the real thing. Ask a child what it's like to be a child, and see what sort of answer you get.

Material that reaches you through other people's stories, or through films and books, is filtered through the consciousness of the original authors and gives you far less sensory detail. A person whose knowledge of snow comes from watching the Winter Games on television is not equipped to convey the sensation of walking through melting snow. A blind writer may not be equipped to communicate nuances of colour. It's a different matter when personal experience is involved: a talented student of mine, who also happens to be blind, opened his description of the scene following a car accident with 'As I stood beside the hot, ticking metal . . .'

There is an exercise that is sometimes given to new writers to help get the creative sap flowing: Make up lists of characters, settings and situations, choose one of each at random, and find a way of fitting them together. The result is sometimes a story.

If you regard the method not as a blueprint but as a mild stimulant to creativity, it can be a useful and entertaining exercise — a bit like an Edwardian parlour game. Making stories out of unconnected events becomes easy once you get the hang of it. I warn you, though, that for new writers it can sometimes be too easy. If you haven't got into the habit of writing with personal involvement, this kind of story-making can turn out to be no more useful than threading plastic beads on a string.

Another way of getting story ideas is to make a list of some personal experiences that you would like to use in a story. You probably have some settings in your memory that appeal to you; a place you dreamed of, or a place where you once played as a child. And you may have a character who interests you lurking at the back of your mind. Your list might look like this:

A milk bar that I remember as a child, smelling of milk and pineapple syrup.
The lost, deserted feeling of my first day at a new school.
A character who is a bit like I was at the age of eleven (but only a bit).
A sad, empty street I remember from somewhere.

And so on. Then go for a walk and let the pieces slide about in your mind.

Since this is a five-finger exercise, something to get you warmed up, it doesn't matter if you don't come back from your walk with a perfectly thought-out story. In fact you almost certainly won't. You might have to move those pieces round for days, weeks or even months, dropping some and adding new ones, before a complete story emerges.

If you stay in a relaxed and receptive mood, eventually story ideas will start collecting. They come together most easily when you don't try hard. Stories aren't made in the logical part of your brain — they're made in the dreaming part, and the more dreaming you do, the better you get at it.

The framework for a practice story isn't hard to find. You can use family reminiscences, jokes, folk tales or myths as the basis for your own story. (In fact the main difference between a story and a myth is that a story exists in the telling, while a myth exists in the events of the story itself, and can be retold many times in many different ways.)

Finding a publishable story idea that is relevant to children is a little more difficult, but only a little. It depends on your skill in other aspects of writing, and your knowledge of children's books in general — things that you'll learn, in part, from later chapters of this book. For now, if you put yourself in story mode for an hour or two a day, using your own inner child as a guide, you will have a wider selection of ideas to choose from, and a better chance of recognising a special idea when it turns up.

When the floating story pieces start coalescing and generating new ones, some writers like to start making notes. You can do this any way you like — it's really just a form of verbal doodling to help you keep track of the developing story. Some writers use diagrams, some write histories for their characters, some collect bits and pieces for a scrap book. Others (I belong to this group) simply sit and write and see what happens. Still others bounce the idea off a sympathetic fellow-writer, or family member, or friend.

The only risky method is the last one. Some people, however much you love them, can in seconds lay the cold hand of death on a story. All they have to say is 'Hasn't it been done before?' or 'That's a cliché, isn't it?' and your infant story is doomed. When you toss the baby to someone, there is only one proper response: to catch it and gently toss it back. Writers know this well, but it's something many non-writers will never understand; they think they are doing you a favour when they point out that the baby has thrown up on its blanket, or that its bottom is wet, or that what you thought was a baby is really only a bundle of rags.

Passion

Look at this piece of writing:

> That day they went to the carnival. They wanted to see some clowns, but there weren't any, so they had a ride. Then they were hungry and thirsty, so they had something to eat and drink.

There is obviously something wrong with it, but what? Before you read any further, try to work out what it is.

I wrote the example especially for this book and its faults are therefore exaggerated, but sooner or later every writer is confronted with a similar piece of writing. Assuming the piece contains plot material that you can't discard, how would you go about fixing it?

Inexperienced writers are apt to remember what they were taught at school, and in an attempt to brighten up the writing they may throw in some adjectives and adverbs, along with some fancier verbs:

> That day they ventured forth to the carnival. They were longing to see the funny clowns, but there weren't any, so they sauntered off to have a ride. Then they were ravenously hungry and thirsty so they wolfed down some delicious food and a lovely cool drink. Then it was late so they journeyed home.

Now it's even worse — still boring, and contrived as well. But what happens if we flesh it out, decorate it a bit more? Does it get any better?

> The bus stopped outside the carnival, and like a huge prehistoric monster spewed its passengers on to the footpath. Alexander and Lydia waited excitedly in the queue with their money. They could hardly wait to see the clowns.

Worse still? Maybe not — but it's certainly no better than the earlier examples. It's still contrived. The bus is nothing like a prehistoric monster, and you would expect a monster to be swallowing people rather than disgorging them; besides, the bus–monster has been done a thousand times before.

It's important to realise that no amount of tinkering with the *writing* is going to improve this passage. There was something missing in the underlying thought, and this has caused a corresponding emptiness in the writing. There was nothing meaningful to say, so the writer didn't say it.

Before you can write any piece of fiction convincingly you must believe in it yourself; you must believe in it so wholeheartedly that sharing it with your readers becomes a compulsion. This degree of intensity comes easily with key scenes — that is why they are key scenes — but when it comes to the others, inventiveness often falters.

A lot of writing is hard work. In between the jam-filled scenes that you want to write — the cliff-top rescue scene, or the disappearance of an important character — are the bread-and-butter scenes that you have to write: the scene that plants the weakened rope, or the scene that gets rid of characters who might be witnesses. Because these bread-and-butter scenes didn't come from your feelings in the first place, they can be difficult to write convincingly.

You can try whipping up some artificial excitement:

That day they were so excited to be going to the carnival! They could hardly wait to see the funny clown! But, oh, dear! When they got to the carnival, there weren't any. What a shame!

As you see, that doesn't work either.

A safer way is to turn the situation over in your mind until you find an aspect that catches your genuine interest. You explore, looking for familiar territory — an aspect of the situation, however tiny, that you feel at home with, that has memories and emotional significance for you.

Sometimes just exploring the setting is enough. Try it. Using your own memories, take yourself to the carnival. Queue up outside, buy your ticket, go through the turnstile. Squeeze through the crowd; listen to the carnival music, the roar and rattle of rides; smell the doughnuts and the hot dogs, the trampled grass and the mud; feel the fine rain on your face. Does anything catch your interest? Often, memories of childhood will come back to you — yourself at the age of one of your characters, running out of money, or getting separated from parents or friends — and you will have found something you can use.

Try this. Sit back in your chair, close your eyes, and imagine you are walking along a beach. Give yourself as much time as you need to complete your stroll, then write down what you noticed. Finish the list before you read on.

Did you write down only visual things — the sun on the water, the colour of the sky, children building dams and sandcastles — or did you include sounds as well? Did you include other perceptions; smell, touch and taste?

If you didn't think of any of these, perhaps you had better go back for another try. Take it a step at a time. How do you arrive? By car? By train or bus? Is anyone with you? What sort of day is it? A chilly Sunday afternoon? A hot Saturday morning? Or a sombre afternoon near the end of summer, with a thunderstorm brewing? You start walking down to the beach. What is your mood? Are you elated, full of holiday joy, or are you a little sad? How would you describe the colours of the sand? How does the sand feel under your feet — cold and gritty, getting into your socks? Or is it hot, scorching your bare feet? Walk down to the water. What does the water feel like on your skin? Look down at your feet in the shallows. What do you see? What do you hear? What can you smell?

As you take yourself on this imaginary walk you may find some surprises. You may find that early on a winter morning, when the sand is cold, the water is unexpectedly warm; or a remembered smell of wet vinyl beach toys may call up childhood holidays.

This walk on the beach is not 'made up' — that is, created out of nothing. You have put it together out of all the other trips to the beach that you remember, both real and fictional. You took the memories from a box labelled 'Beach', cut them into pieces, and recombined them. That's imagination.

When you work with your own memories you find that they come with feeling already attached, and this feeling passes into the writing. You may also notice that you do better if you don't hurry. It takes time to get deep enough into a setting to start recreating it.

A wise editor once gave me an excellent piece of advice; it sounds dangerously like a rule, but I am going to pass it on to you anyway: *Every scene must have either warmth or conflict*. It's not strictly true for all cases — other feelings, such as fear or suspense, will work as well as conflict, but the point the editor was making is that every scene should have at least one important emotion running through it. This is impossible if you don't care about what you are writing — care about it so much that in a sense it becomes true. E. M. Forster called this *passion* (and the lack of it John Gardner called *frigidity*). That is why the sort of exercise described on page 8 (the sort where you mix random elements to generate a story idea) will not always produce good writing.

It takes time to create a setting from the places in your memory, and a setting grows in intensity and detail as you work with it. You have probably discovered this for yourself; if you decided to follow your characters to a fairy-floss stall you had to put one there for them; if they asked directions from someone selling hot dogs you had to imagine not only the stall but the hot-dog seller too.

In the early stages of a piece of writing the only thing you have to guide you is your feeling about what you have written. It is important to learn how it feels when you are getting it right. The five-finger exercises in this book will help you to recognise that feeling.

2 LASTING THE DISTANCE

Without reading any further, take a look at the following situations. Write about fifty words describing a character involved in each activity.

> Brushing teeth
> Driving a train
> Planning a bank robbery

Put the writing aside. You'll come back to it later.

Writing is a matter of sharing feelings and perceptions rather than just telling readers about them. To be worth sharing, these perceptions need to be your own. (If you don't believe me, ask someone to tell you the story of the video they watched last night, and see how gripping you find it.)

The world changes. Knitting needles, being made of different materials, make a different sound than they made fifty or even thirty years ago. So do sewing machines, trains, planes, lifts, televisions, clocks, refrigerators, typewriters, razors, racing cars and telephones. Of course it's unlikely you'd make a mistake with something you know, such as a telephone; but before you forget and write 'the click-clack of busy needles' or 'the roar of racing cars' because that's how another writer once described them, think. Listen! They probably sound quite different now.

The aim of fiction is not to make readers believe it is true (in which case we leave the realms of fiction and enter the realms of fraud) but to make them believe it *could* be true. Children read a work of fiction knowing that it isn't true, but they join in the game of Let's Imagine with the author. They slip between the words and enter the world of the story, and while they are there, they allow themselves to believe completely.

Creating this story world and holding the reader in it is part of the skill of writing — and it seems to be the part that non-writers find so mysterious, as if the imagination were indeed a secret place where it all came from. But whether it is a classroom in 2160, or a cafe in 1880, or the back seat of the family car in 1990, if a setting is to be believable it must be put together out of building blocks from your memory.

For this reason there is no such thing as an 'imaginative' setting. A setting is either realised or it isn't. The mythical world of Tharg, with its double purple shadows and green and gold sunsets, is no easier or more difficult to create than an ice-cream parlour in Brisbane or a laundromat in Perth.

You probably remember reading a book in which something that was awkward, or glaringly untrue, or improbable, jolted you out of your credulity. If the book was otherwise good you tried to forget this lapse and carried on believing and enjoying. But a story that has too many such lapses becomes unreadable; the illusion is spoilt for us.

A warning sign that you should heed is the feeling that you don't believe what you are writing. You may feel that it is all very remote and unimportant. Leon Garfield once talked of 'writing several inches above the paper'; others have mentioned 'writing through a sheet of glass'. But it amounts to the same thing — the writer is not making contact with that basic material, the store of personal experience.

This doesn't mean you are limited to sailing round and round your own backyard pool, endlessly plumbing known, shallow depths. Voyages of discovery are still possible if you look at fictitious experiences by the light of real ones. For example, it is not necessary to fall over a cliff yourself in order to tell your reader what it is like. Instead you can draw on your own related experiences: memories of lesser falls and of times when you nearly fell, and memories of sudden fright. Wherever possible you will tailor your character's fall to fit your own experience, and so get a more vivid and believable result.

Let's have a look at the exercise you did — the three situations. First, brushing teeth. The likely problem here was that you just couldn't find anything interesting to write about. You have cleaned your teeth almost every day of your life, and you might feel there's not much to be said about it. Perhaps you got round the problem by personifying the toothpaste or the toothbrush, but the result doesn't seem to ring true — it's hard to believe in a talking toothbrush. (I mean *passionately* believe — to the point where you walk into the bathroom to clean your teeth, and for an instant wonder if the toothbrush is annoyed with you.)

Or perhaps, in spite of the warning in the last chapter, you tried to make up for the piece's general lack by choosing striking, vivid words; but it still doesn't seem right.

To make the piece work you needed to add an emotional dimension. Try this variation. You are eleven years old. A little while ago you heard that your father, who is an orthodontist, has moved out of the family home and gone to live with his nurse. Now it is bedtime and you are cleaning your teeth. Describe the scene, but without mentioning your father, his profession, or his nurse.

I'm willing to bet that this version is easier to write — or at least more interesting.

Perhaps the second situation, driving a train, seemed to offer more possibilities, but the problem was finding anything to write about at all. You have never in your life driven a train and there seemed to be nothing to go on. If you look now at what you have written, it may seem oddly bare and empty — a cardboard set, with the controls of a train crudely painted on.

Here, too, you may have tried to conceal the problem with language. But even with rich language you may still not feel convinced; and if you aren't convinced, who else will be?

But there were chances here too. You could have put yourself in the position of someone who knows nothing about driving a train and is about to learn. You might have drawn on your experiences of driving lessons perhaps, or even piano lessons — and coupled these with what you know about trains as a passenger. Or you could have invented a new kind of train, one that you do know about because you invented it. As with the last example, you need an underlying mood or emotion.

The third situation had a quality that the other two lacked: it was inherently exciting. That could have made it easier to write about, but there was still plenty of room for trouble. You might have found that you knew as little about robbing banks as you did about driving trains. The difference is that you have seen plenty of fictionalised bank robberies. If you are old enough, you may also have read about them in children's books. You know the sort of thing — how four children and a dog foil the bank robbers, win a reward and are home in time for tea.

Did you succumb to temptation and discard your own experience as irrelevant? Did you put your bank robbery together out of bits of old films and undistinguished books? Unless you used a strong underpinning of fact (perhaps drawing on familiar situations, locations and people) and unless you thought the situation through as it might occur in real life, we could be back to the cardboard sets again. One way of looking at this situation (did it occur to you?) would be through the eyes of a child who is not aware of what is going on. In certain essential ways, is planning a bank robbery any different from planning any other kind of enterprise? Do bank robbers look different from anybody else? Of course not — they look like doctors, plumbers and teachers, just as doctors, plumbers and teachers sometimes look like bank robbers.

If you remembered this, full marks. Or did you put the bank robbers in a hideout, and give them names like Shifty, Fred and Scarface?

The easiest way to make a situation like this convincing is to ignore the films and books and concentrate instead on what you know to be true. If you construct your scene out of the bits and pieces of memory that you have stored away, you can still enjoy the voyage of discovery. If the raw material has an underpinning of truth it will also have an emotional dimension. The imagined world will be convincing, and satisfying to write about.

Things can go wrong

Right at the beginning of a piece of writing, at the point where fact becomes fiction, new writers find their first difficulty. Some beginners feel that if they are going to use their own experience they should record it exactly as it happened; changing it, even in minuscule ways, feels like cheating. This tyranny of real-life truth over fictional truth can cause its own kind of trouble: a story tied down like this can't fly. It can be interesting or even moving as an autobiographical record, but it will never take you on a voyage of discovery, and it will never reveal meaning.

If when you write you find that real-life events are reproducing themselves on the page exactly as they happened, clipping the story's wings, there are at least two remedies you can try. One is to put the story idea away until you find another idea — or more ideas — to blend with it. This thickening process seems to happen quite naturally over time, even when you're not aware of it, and nearly always leads to a better story.

Another way of liberating your story is to change some of the facts into fiction. If the event took place on a hot afternoon, try a cold night instead; if the story is set in a city, try moving it to the country. This sort of change forces you to imagine instead of merely remembering — you are forced to put various remembered elements together and make a synthesis. When this happens the process of imagination has begun and the story is on its way.

Now you can let yourself fantasise: how else could the story events have turned out? Suppose that person had been a woman instead of a man? Suppose she got there five minutes later? and so on. The only thing about the original story that you should try to keep intact is the feeling; but even that can be changed if you like. It's your story.

If the experience you propose using is recent, and also dramatic or painful, it can sometimes overwhelm you, causing you merely to describe it when what you really wanted was to discover some transcendent meaning. The answer is probably to leave this experience alone for a while, until you are ready to use it. In Rilke's words, experience must 'enter the poet's bone and blood' before it becomes available. 'It is not enough to have memories. One must have vast patience until they come again.'

If the story needs coaxing along, you can ask it questions; these should take the form of gentle prompting rather than all-out grilling. While you are in a relaxed frame of mind, put yourself in the place of an interested listener and tell the story to yourself, or watch it as a film. Ask yourself 'If all this had really happened, exactly how would it have happened?' or 'How did this situation come about?' The relaxed frame of mind is the key. Most writers find that if they sit down with the express purpose of thinking up a story it simply doesn't happen. But if you go for a walk, peel some potatoes, do some washing up or cut the grass while you play around with your questions, you might have better luck.

3 CHARACTERS

Good children's stories are about people rather than events or ideas, a fact that puts characters right at the heart of story telling. For many writers, a story can't even begin to come together until the character whose story it is has been created. There are many ways of doing this, and the only right one is the one that works best for you. Some characters are put together one attribute at a time. Others, like Minerva, spring fully formed from their creators' foreheads. But one thing all fiction writers seem to agree on: a character's name is specially significant.

Names

There has always been a kind of magic attached to names. In many folk traditions, to let a sorcerer know your true name was to put yourself in danger — anyone who knew your true name had power over you. Writers, being sorcerers of a kind, know that this works in fiction too: once you know a character's true name it becomes your character and will do your bidding.

When you set out to create a character you are not necessarily setting out to create a detailed, real person; if that were true, characters could be derived from psychology text books and writers would be out of a job. What you are aiming at is a character whom readers will believe in and care about, and that is not necessarily the same as a real person.

The believability of a character depends firstly on your perceptions of yourself, and to a lesser extent on your observation of other people. Your ideas and feelings, your understanding of your own self, are the key to understanding the behaviour of your characters. In essence, your major characters are yourself: they are aspects of your own personality which you recognise and 'wear' while you are writing. Because human beings share essential characteristics (otherwise psychologists would be out of a job too) your readers recognise the characters and believe in them.

You could say that your major characters already exist within you, and it is naming them that brings them forward. This might explain the curious process that many writers go through when they start a new book. Nothing can begin until the major characters are named, and a name has to be a character's true name, not just a pseudonym to fill the gap until a better sounding one turns up.

Naming characters can take longer than you'd think. You can spend days looking through telephone books and What to Name the Baby books, school rolls or even, as some writers have recommended, atlases, without finding the right one. Sometimes names have to be made up. When you do find the name you know instantly that it is the right one; it's as if the character, recognising that their true name has been spoken, steps forward.

That's why you find so few Johns and Marys in fiction. Instead you find Africa, Dicey, Callie, Martin Chuzzlewit and the Reverend Snape — names that meant something to their creator.

When naming characters there is one class of names you should think twice about, and that is playful, made-up names like Mrs Wigglewoggle or Mr Roly Jolyon Kondobulom. They are fun, and children enjoy them, but take care. Characters with nonsense names are fine if nonsense is your intention, especially if the names include a play on words, such as Walter de la Mare's verse:

> In a dear little house
> Which I shared with my Fanny
> Lived a dear little mouse
> And we called it
> Magnani.

If you think names really don't make much difference, have a look at these two versions of the same story opening:

Mrs Wigglewoggle's husband died a long time ago. Now she lived with her dog. His name was Barkalot. Barkalot loved Mrs Wigglewoggle . . .

And this is the original version:

'Rose's husband died a long time ago. Now she lived with her dog. His name was John Brown. John Brown loved Rose . . .'

Characters come in two categories. In longer fiction, the main character is usually one who, if we put them in another situation, can reveal another dimension of themselves. In a picture book, or in a short novel with several characters, there isn't time to draw each one as a fully rounded person. So the minor characters, and sometimes even major ones, are constructed as two-dimensional figures — cardboard cut-outs that can be moved about as you need them. These characters don't develop, or change, or make us wonder about them; they are what they seem to be and what you see is what you get.

This doesn't mean that they have to be badly drawn. The casual people who move in and out of your stories — the bus drivers, teachers, holiday-makers, cashiers, gardeners, parents or chemists who deliver messages, reveal plot points or add colour — still need to be believable. But where we might get to know a round character a bit at a time, these characters are usually revealed to us instantly.

There is a way of turning a flat character into a round one, as long as you are subtle about it. (Being unsubtle leads you into clichés like the tragic clown, or the prostitute with a heart of gold.) You do it by putting together contradictory characteristics — the second characteristic has to be one that surprises us. You bend and stretch the character to accommodate the new attribute, and when the two fit into the one character, there you have it — the character has become round.

Each of the following flat characters has done something to surprise us.

Sister Angelica, a sweet and devout young nun who looks after the convent chickens, has been caught harbouring an escaped convict (a failed property developer) in the hen house.

Dr Oswald Jeffries, the stern headmaster of Saint Martin's Collegiate School for Young Gentlemen (also known as 'Hanging' Jeffries) has been caught stealing from the poor box.

Lydia Lovepenny is the indulged only daughter of a corrupt government official. Famous as a society and fashion figure, she is said to own over 1000 white fur dressing-gowns with slippers to match. Recently she has been caught secretly donating large amounts of money to Greenpeace.

Without taking any moral position over what these characters have done — without even mentioning it — and without resorting to caricature, imagine yourself as friend and confidant of each one, and try to explain them as characters.

I was going to be really cruel and say 'in fifty words or less', but you see what I mean. To explain complexities like this will take more than a few words; it is the stuff whole stories are made of. The big difference between round characters and flat ones is that the possibilities of the flat ones *can* be summed up 'in fifty words or less', while round ones, like real people, are capable of development.

Some beginning writers tend to use cardboard characters everywhere, even as central characters in novels, and disguise them as round ones by sticking two of them together, like this:

All the reader knows of Desley is that she is fourteen and wants to be a nurse. 'Hm,' says her author. 'She sounds a bit wimpish. Let's give her a physical dimension.' And so the girl becomes a trapeze artist as well. But there is no contradiction implied; the character needs no explanation or adjustment; and so Desley is still flat — only now she is a flat trapeze artist as well.

Describing characters

At the beginning of a new story it's tempting to start with a description of the main characters. It has a businesslike feel to it, and gives a writer the impression that the story has begun:

Zack was ten years old. He had blue eyes, freckles, and sandy-fair hair that stuck out all over. His brother Toby was a year younger. He had dark hair, a round face, and brown eyes.

This would not be particularly rivetting in any story, but in a children's story it is deadly. (I am assuming that Zack's appearance plays no part in the story — that he is not kidnapped in mistake for someone else, for example.) Children don't need to have characters described for them in this way — they visualise better than many adults do. Since stories and novels intended for children are shorter than those intended for adults, you have no words to waste. If your readers are very young and need help to visualise the characters, ask the publisher to arrange illustrations for you.

There is also a good reason for not being too specific about a character's age. When one day an eleven-year-old, picking up a favourite book, reads 'Zack was ten years old', that may be the end of the favourite book. Children find it hard to identify with someone younger than they are; without that mention of his age, Zack might have gone on giving pleasure for another three or four years.

So instead of using up valuable space to tell us what central characters look like, it is more useful to show us what they *are* like. Ideally we should find this out from watching the characters and noticing what they say and do. While we are doing that, the story is also moving forward.

When the narrator tells us that Zack is ten years old and has freckles you have to hold up the story to do it. But if you let us see that he shares a bedroom with Toby, and that Zack has drawn a line down the middle of the room and won't allow Toby's clutter to cross it; that Zack keeps his own things in neat piles and counts them often to make sure they are still there — then the story is already beginning. With the information we have been given a picture has emerged, and a story possibility is emerging with it.

If it's important to you to describe your characters you can still do it, but don't hold up the story for it. In a children's book there is nothing more important than the story — not even the messages it carries.

There will be times when a character's appearance is important to the story. In this case you can use the appearance of the characters to show what they are like:

'a dirty slipshod girl in black cotton stockings' (*The Pickwick Papers*, Charles Dickens)

or:

'There were two women opposite him, a fat one and a thin one, and they talked without stopping, smacking their lips in between sentences and seeming to enjoy what they said as much as if it were something to eat.' (*The Children of Green Knowe*, L. M. Boston)

But trying to sneak in a description of a character while the story is running can lead to some particular awkwardnesses:

'I think we should go to the beach,' said Luke.
Alison spun round as if she had just discovered the short athletic boy. 'Don't be silly.'

The writer's intention is plain enough; we are meant to understand that Luke is short, athletic and a boy. But it doesn't quite come out like that. It sounds as if Alison, working away in a government laboratory somewhere, has just discovered The Short Athletic Boy, which (when fitted with a Wankel Rotary Engine) will revolutionise the transport industry.

There can be other problems with sneaked-in descriptions:

Timothy swung his short fat legs out of bed.

Whether this works or not depends on where the narrator has decided to stand. If the narrator is standing across the room from Timothy there is no problem; Timothy's legs may be just as noteworthy as anything else in the room. But what if the narrator is inside Timothy's head? In this case it sounds as if Timothy is observing his own legs. This may be just what you had in mind — perhaps there is something unusual about them today. But if there isn't, readers have a right to feel irritated. The author has shoved the narrator aside, and clumsily broken into the story to tell us something we didn't need to know.

> Susannah sat by the lattice where the dry leaves of the choko vine rustled; she waited. She felt irritated; four o'clock, and no one had come. She was a tall, ungainly girl of thirteen.

As you can see, the opening sentences are all right, but there's something very wrong with the last sentence in the paragraph. Even if you make 'She was a tall girl of thirteen' into the start of a new paragraph, it still jars.

The problem has to do with viewpoint, the sudden shift from being on the inside with Susannah to being on the outside, looking at her. (The jump in the other direction doesn't bother us nearly as much. Try transposing the two sections and see. There's more about this in Chapter 7.)

Years ago writers used to get round this difficulty by hanging a mirror somewhere handy. Then they used to manoeuvre the character towards it:

> Susannah sat by the lattice where the dry leaves of the choko vine rustled; she waited. She felt irritated; four o'clock, and no one had come.
>
> She paced the veranda, walking up and down its length, past the bedrooms where the french windows stood open. She glanced into the rooms as she passed. In one, she saw a movement: it was herself, reflected in an oval mirror that stood beside the bed. She was surprised to see how tall and ungainly she had grown.

Some writers consider the mirror to be a tired old device, not worth using, but many others go on using it successfully (and unobtrusively).

Stereotypes

Television is a potent influence on children's writers. If you forget to use your personal knowledge as a base for your characters, you can find yourself reaching out for what seems to be the next best thing — a world, complete with characters, that already exists, right there in front of your eyes: Televisionland.

You can tell when you are in Televisionland instead of your own world by the boring wholesomeness of the stereotypes. These aren't perpetuated because they are good, or because children like them, or because writers suffer from an invincible form of moral turpitude. It's because everyone feels safer doing something that has been done successfully before. In television this might even work (why else would anyone want to remake Skippy?) but fortunately it's not true in children's books.

However, the yearning for safety does sometimes lure new writers into strange places. There is a recurring motif among stories by new writers, an odd phenomenon: most choose a boy as their central character. It's even odder when you consider that more than half these writers are women, and many of them are feminists.

I don't mean that writers should only write about the gender they were born into. But if you are a woman, and you find yourself automatically weaving stories round boys, and never girls, perhaps you should ask yourself why. Experienced writers should be able to work with characters of both sexes, and any in between; but for many women writers, the first story they write about a girl is a milestone in their development. The first good story about a boy may be another. The same thing might also be said about male writers, who could find themselves in the opposite situation.

In recent years there has been an increased clamour for stories that show girls 'in active roles'. Writers have hauled themselves, muttering, onto the bandwagon, with results similar to those you'd expect if there were a clamour for giraffe stories: lots of stories in which the giraffe isn't really a giraffe but some other animal in disguise; lots of stories in which the giraffe is more important than the story; and one or two good stories about a giraffe.

It must be tempting, for those who deal with children, to see the literature of children as a means of influencing and controlling their opinions — just as our Victorian forebears did. But I like to think that one day it will dawn on all children's book experts, not just the enlightened ones, that writers aren't slot machines; that good stories, ones that last, are still about people and about being human.

To give you some practice in creating a character, here are two exercises you can try.

Imagine yourself as the wolf from the story of Little Red Riding Hood. In your own (i.e. the wolf's) words, explain to a group of children who know the story just why you ate Red Riding Hood's grandmother. You can choose how old the children are, but you must sound utterly convincing.

Invent an adult character and tell us about that character from a child's point of view. (You will need to decide beforehand how old the child is.) If this exercise goes well, you may find you are writing transparently, where readers are able to read through one interpretation of the events and perceive another one underneath it.

However you go about creating your characters, there are a couple of things you need to look out for:

Sentimentality

By this I mean the sugary, patronising tenderness that some writers are tempted into when they write about babies, animals, mothers, grandmothers, young children, or aged war veterans. But if you agree that your characters are yourself, you will give them more respect.

Author's bias

Unless you have a particular reason for it, (after all, you are the author and it's your business) be careful about deciding whether a character is 'good' or 'bad'. It's true that there are unpleasant people around; but no one actually rubs their hands and says 'Aha! Today I think I'll go out and do some evil'. (Though come to think of it, a character who did would be quite entertaining.) In a well-drawn character, what we think of as 'bad' is more likely to be a perversion of some quality that we admire, or an innocent quality carried to excess.

The same goes for characters you might think of as 'good': a supporting mother who is philosophically opposed to collecting benefits, and who therefore lives in poverty, could be an interesting character to explore. But if we discover that the author admires the character unreservedly, and is trying to persuade us to feel the same way, we will stop caring about them. We might even look round for someone bad to barrack for.

Settings as characters

I'll finish this chapter by pointing out an oddity: a setting is a character too. A setting in a longer story (in a picture book the setting is created by the illustrator) should be more than a mere backdrop to the action. In the very best stories the landscape emerges as a presence in its own right, and exerts an influence on the characters. You can see this in Tove Jansson's *Moominpappa at Sea* as well as in Graham Greene's *The Power and the Glory*; in both books the characters are inseparable from their setting.

Just as your characters emerge from within you, so do the significant parts of your settings. Even though stories are about people, you may find that your response to a remembered or imagined landscape is what starts the story process.

4 A MATTER OF STYLE

Every writer has pet phrases, familiar expressions and favourite rhythms. This is a matter of individual taste and quite legitimate — it's impossible to write any other way. But allowing for differences in personal voice, there are things you should watch out for in your writing: clumsiness, clichés, redundancies, inappropriate grandeur, archaic expressions, inappropriate imagery, and accidental music to name just a few.

Clumsiness

Beginning writers often overlook clumsiness, which usually takes the form of a lot of little faults rather than a few dramatically big ones. But like all writing faults, they are cumulative; you can get away with one or two, but several can cast a veil over the writing, eventually making it unreadable. Fortunately it works the other way too: the removal of many small roughnesses can make a startling improvement to clarity and vividness.

Getting things in their wrong order is a form of clumsiness. My father, who was fond of quoting Cobbett, used to say 'Sit down to write what you have thought, and not to think what you shall write.' But thoughts don't always occur in chronological order: The first draft of your narrative may present events in the order in which you thought of them, rather than in the order in which they would happen. Like this:

> They dived into the river, squeezing through the bushes which tore their clothes.

Writers often work backwards in this way. The idea of diving into the river occurred first, but when the writer visualised the river the bushes appeared too, and then the torn clothes. Sometimes whole strings of elements appear as the writer explores further and further back:

They dived into the river, squeezing through the bushes which tore their clothes that had been bought only a week ago when Mrs Dinkel realised how much the children had grown.

No one would have any trouble guessing what the writer meant, which is why beginners sometimes forget to revise sentences like this. But a good writer doesn't expect readers — especially child readers — to guess. The words have to be transparent, so that without any conscious effort we find ourselves slipping through them, like Alice through the looking-glass, into the world of the story.

Try it. Rewrite the above events in their proper order, and see how the picture comes into focus.

Cluttered sentences are another form of clumsiness. Children's writers are usually advised to keep their sentences short, but there is more to it than that; old school readers had short sentences, but many of them still made dull reading. On the other hand, look at this long sentence:

'Rosie the hen went for a walk across the yard around the pond over the haycock past the mill through the fence under the beehive and got back in time for dinner.' (*Rosie's Walk*, Pat Hutchins)

Even without the illustrations we have a clear picture of everything that Rosie is doing. (Although we need to look at the illustrations to see what the fox is doing!)

That long sentence works because it isn't cluttered. It is following one idea — Rosie's walk — and each element is an aspect of that walk.

Now look at this long sentence:

Rupert the grey rock wallaby hopped nimbly down from his spot on top of the smooth round rocks beside the river.

What are we to imagine — the rock wallaby hopping nimbly, his spot on the rocks, the shape and texture of the rocks, the river, or the rocks beside the river? The sentence is so cluttered that we can't decide; we end up with no picture at all, except perhaps of some rocks and a scrap of grey fur.

If you have trouble paring your sentences down to children's length, aim at sentences that work with one idea at a time. Anything you want to add that isn't part of that idea is probably better with a sentence of its own, or even a separate paragraph.

Don't bother about fancy word order or fancy constructions. Just use your ordinary everyday speaking voice.

Bundles of words are a form of clumsiness. Most children's writers have no trouble avoiding concatenations of polysyllabic verbalisations because usually we write the way we speak. But bundles of short words, like prepositions and pronouns, can be a problem:

She gave it to him, and then he cut it up and gave it back to her.

The problem is not so much the words themselves, but that they are all of one syllable; they produce heavy, knocking rhythms that make the narrative sound as if it has got stuck behind a door. The remedy is either to leave out some words, or change some of the pronouns to longer names, or recast the sentence.

Clichés

There are times when writing for children seems to bring out the worst in us; the restricted vocabulary strangles us. Some days we despair and grab whatever comes to hand — whatever sounds safe and familiar, or has been sanctified by use. On these bad days characters run as fast as their legs can carry them, rise early and dress hurriedly in clothes that are somewhat the worse for wear, and say things excitedly. When they are troubled they frown, or bite their lip, but at other times they may manage a smile — or a smile may play round the corners of their mouth — and their eyes may shine, sparkle, dance or twinkle.

Everyone lapses like this occasionally. The above examples were all found in recently published books, some of them award winners whose authors had nodded off on Mount Olympus. But you should recognise that they are indeed lapses, and not the sort of writing to aim for.

Beginning writers are especially drawn to clichés. A cliché is a cliché because it was a vivid, striking expression in the first place, which is why it has been used so often. If the expression has been in print so often, you might be tempted to think there is something special about it, a sort of Good Writing Institute Seal of Approval. But the earlier part of this book should have warned you off. As an apprentice writer you should get into the habit of trusting your own perceptions and your own voice. Instead of falling into the trap of using clichés you will be able to avoid them like the plague . . .

And having said that, I must also tell you that sometimes a cliché is exactly the expression you need. But it should be there by choice, not by misadventure.

Redundancies

Most writers, as they think their way into what they are writing, say the same thing several different ways. That is part of the writing process. It's a bit like choosing clothes; you can see them on the rack and know which ones will probably suit, but you can't be sure till you try them on. Unedited writing usually contains a pile of words and sentences that didn't suit quite as well as some others, and removing them is part of the writing process too.

Beginning writers often find it hard to cut material. Writing can be hard work; when words have been squeezed out of you like drops from a dry lemon you are entitled to feel some attachment to them. Nevertheless, just the same, and notwithstanding, if you want your writing to make its point and if it is to convey the meaning you want, and communicate with the reader, it's better to say things only once. Or two or three times at the very most.

'Excited' and 'excitedly' are so often redundant in children's books that I would like to see them rested altogether for a good hundred years. 'Excitedly' certainly doesn't belong in sentences like '"Here comes Father Christmas" shouted Timothy excitedly'. Words are so scarce in children's books that you can't afford to waste a single one. Shouting is already a sign of excitement, of arousal, so there is no need for 'excitedly'.

There is another reason for leaving it out. When you write for children you should resist trying to do their imagining for them: telling children how everything looks, what colour it is, and the tone of voice in which everything is said is a form of adult control. It's a kind of condescension, a big sin in children's books, and it's easy to see why. If you keep telling children how to think and feel, instead of giving them the freedom to discover things for themselves, you are not treating them as equals in the reader–writer partnership: you are treating them as puppets.

Inappropriate grandeur

You expect a judgment from the High Court or a ruling from a government minister to be written in more elevated language than a letter from a friend. What you don't expect is to see the levels mixed up:

> The Minister has ruled that a person may, in certain circumstances, nick off overseas without in any way affecting his or her entitlements.

The sudden shift in style level is easy to see here, but it may not be when it happens in the opposite direction, which is more likely. Inexperienced writers sometimes feel tempted to translate everyday words into grander ones in the belief that their writing will seem more distinguished. So car may be changed into vehicle, buy into purchase, get into receive, give into donate, want into wish, go into venture, and so on.

All sorts of narrative voices are possible, and you are allowed to have a grand one if you like. But take care to sustain it. This isn't always easy; if you are not using a voice that comes naturally to you, there is a risk that now and then the voice will slip and the style will fall flat on its face — the narrative equivalent of the pompous man on the banana skin.

If you do want to use grand words, make sure they mean what you think they mean. To peruse a book and to read it, for example, are not the same thing; and 'venture' is not a straight swap for 'go'. The usual reason a language has more than one word for something is that the words are *not* interchangeable, and therefore provide a useful distinction. When two words do mean exactly the same thing they don't coexist for long; the tendency is for one of them to change its meaning or disappear.

Children's writers are particularly tempted towards grand words. Inside each one of us is a bossy teacher who feels that mere entertainment is a waste of time, and that we should really be extending children's vocabularies and improving their minds. Elevated style in children's narrative (while it may impress some adults) produces a peculiar effect; it is as if the comfortable, floppy-hatted story-teller we are used to has turned into a thin-lipped Victorian governess, who raps our knuckles and tells us to sit up straight. If the style is not appropriate to the characters and the story, and if it is not accessible to child readers, it can drive all the fun out of reading.

Archaic expressions

I mean words like *forth*, *perchance*, *nigh*, *save* (instead of *except*), *rive* (usually seen as its past participle, *riven*), *rend*, *peradventure*, *ere*, *oft*, and so on. This sort of language is closely related to the grand style I referred to above, and sometimes the two are found together.

Archaic language does have a place, when it is used by a character or narrator from whom we expect it. But archaic expressions sprinkled into a present-day narrative do nothing to improve it. Venturing forth to do some shopping sounds no more flavourful than merely going shopping; 'When death was nigh they sang hymns' sounds no more noble than singing hymns when death is only near.

Archaic words can cause the writing to lose immediacy; because they are so unfamiliar, these words keep us at arm's length. Language is a means, an instrument. Its best use is in making interesting ideas transparent, rather than making transparent ideas sound interesting.

Inappropriate imagery

In good writing, imagery is an integral part of what is being said; it's the clearest, simplest way the author could find to let us know what something was like. The deeper and more personal the writer's original perception, the fresher and more gratifying the image is likely to be.

Because original ideas and striking images are often found together in good writing, it has led some beginning writers into a fallacy: the belief that the striking images are what made the writing good. But images have to serve a purpose. If they don't, they are no more than curlicues and arabesques embellishing the writing, and no matter how startling they are you are better off without them. The following simile is certainly startling:

A volley of arrows flew over the lake like a flock of dangerous ducks.

But you can hear the machinery clanking. The image is a circular one. We associate ducks with comfortable things like eggs, dinner tables, comic strips, picture books and the children's bath time; although ducks fly in formation and have feathers, the resemblance to arrows ends there. To force the comparison to make some kind of sense the author needed a closer, more telling similarity. But there wasn't one; and so the author borrowed 'dangerous' from 'arrows' and stuck it onto 'ducks'. The result is a flock of quacking birds that it's safer not to stand under. Compare this with John Clare's cranes:

'Cranking their jarring melancholy cry through the long journey of the cheerless sky.'

Another kind of inappropriate image results when a writer, searching for something interesting to say about an inanimate object, finally gives up and pretends for a moment that it's human, or at least sentient:

The necklace nestled happily in a drawer, resisting all efforts to find it.

This sort of imagery was allowable a hundred or so years ago, but fashions change. Telling us that a necklace 'nestles', as a child or a small furry animal might do, or that it could be happy, or could deliberately resist being found, in no way increases our understanding of this necklace or of necklaces in general. We don't catch our breath and cry 'Yes! That's just how necklaces are!' Like the earlier example, this image does nothing except decorate the text, and for this reason it's better left out.

And because there has to be an exception, I must point out that Douglas Adams (*The Hitch Hikers' Guide to the Galaxy*) frequently uses personification for humorous effect.

'Marvin ignored him.

"You watch this door," he muttered, "it's about to open again. I can tell by the intolerable air of smugness it suddenly generates."

With an ingratiating little whine the door slid open again and Marvin stomped through.'

And that's a good reason not to use it when you are being serious.

Accidental music

Even if a story isn't being read aloud, readers still hear the words in their heads. Anything that is awkward to say will stick out unpleasantly: tongue-twisters; unintentional correspondences, rhymes or assonances; lumpy rhythms, and bundles of prepositions:

They headed off down the track towards the lagoon.

It pains me to admit it, but this example comes from my own work. As if the bumping monosyllables — off down the track — weren't bad enough, I compounded my sin by adding yet another preposition. These days I'd probably remove the entire sentence and pick the characters up at the lagoon.

Why is it that when you absolutely must have a rhyme (say for 'orange') there is none to be found, but when you want to avoid words that sound similar they pop up all over the place?

The origin of oranges is to be found in Norwich.

They arranged the oranges in a porringer.

She screamed; she had never seen such a scene.

They pushed through the bushes with a whoosh!

Awkwardnesses like these can work against good story-telling, drawing attention to the words just when you want them to disappear. But one way of avoiding such accidental music is to read your work aloud. Another is to imagine you are reading it aloud — not quite as good as the first, but better than nothing.

Rhythm can cause problems. All good writing has it, either large and rolling, like the incantatory rhythms of Greek drama, or the subtle speech rhythms of Katherine Paterson, and many talented beginners write naturally and rhythmically without even thinking about it. Rhythm is as important in prose as it is in poetry, and it has the same purpose: to put particular words in stressed or unstressed positions, so that meaning can be modified, clarified or strengthened.

The old opening of *Star Trek* included the words 'to boldly go where no man has gone before'. The rhythm of the line put 'man' in a stressed position, and the line itself, because of that slight gap at 'no man' (where the rhythm is interrupted) lent itself to being spoken slowly and weightily, and Trekkies loved it.

The need for non-sexist language led to a change. In a new series, the writers exchanged 'man' for a shorter syllable, 'one'. But the new version doesn't have quite the same ring as the old one. The difference is that you can't stress 'one' the way you could stress 'man', with its longer vowel. We hear the voice intone 'To boldly go where no one has gone before', and now the line seems more funny than weighty.

Small points, but don't ever think they are small enough to overlook. Good or indifferent writing depends on your attitude to such details.

5 SOME WORDS ON LANGUAGE

Writers, being custodians of the language, are allowed to break the rules now and then. There is more than one standard of correctness in language, and ultimately correctness simply means the form of language that most people in a given group use. But it's one thing to use an extraordinary form of language because you have decided it is clearer, and quite another to use it because you don't understand what you are doing.

Children's writers are prone to a particular kind of error. Because the schoolteacher in us is only just below the surface, sometimes we err not by breaking old rules, but by inventing new, unnecessary ones.

If I were you

One example is the use of the subjunctive mood. The subjunctive mood is a form of the verb that tells us that the writer has stopped dealing in those real matters you can argue about ('The Queen is alive', 'Matthew is here') and has started dealing in uncertainties like wishes, commands, and unreal situations ('Long live the Queen', 'If only Matthew were here').

The most important thing you need to know about this form is that it is gradually disappearing. In ordinary speech you are more likely to hear 'I wish I was going' or 'If only it was Saturday', than 'I wish I were going' or 'If only it were Saturday'. The subjunctive is invited to the party mainly for old times' sake, which is why we keep using familiar but fossilised expressions like 'Be that as it may' or 'If I were you'.

Since children's stories are usually written in an everyday speaking voice, the subjunctive is rare: 'Hubert found the party so boring that he began to wish he were at home' is much less common than 'he began to wish he was at home'; or it should be. But because those unreal conditions and vestigial 'weres' are so often introduced by 'if' ('if I were king') some writers salivate at the sight of any 'if' at all, and don't feel right until they have added a 'were', even if it doesn't make sense:

He asked if it were her birthday.

If he were German, you couldn't tell from his accent.

Even in the subjunctive's heyday it would never have been used like this. Both examples should have the ordinary form, 'was'. The difference is that these 'ifs' are not introducing hypothetical situations, and so 'were' is stilted and unnatural — and wrong.

As a writer, it's your job to know about language — what is considered correct at the moment, and what isn't. When you aren't sure, it is far safer, and far kinder to your young readers, to come down on the side of everyday speech.

They and them and he and him and her

One of the problems with English is that we have no pronoun corresponding to 'anyone' in sentences like 'If anyone calls, tell (that person) I'll be back soon'. We can be logical and grammatical and specify whether to 'tell him' or 'tell her', but that excludes one gender. Because the notion of purely grammatical gender is foreign to us, we take matters of gender very seriously.

One way out of it is to use our common sense and say 'If anyone calls, tell them I'll be back soon', which is what people did until nineteenth-century grammarians decided they were wrong.

The grammarians pointed out the inconsistency, and presumed wrongness, of using a plural pronoun to refer to a singular noun; they overlooked the inconsistency of using a masculine pronoun to refer to females as well as males. Ordinary users of language believed them, quite forgetting that what is important about language is not whether it follows a tidy pattern, but whether it does its job of conveying ideas. And so in deferring to the grammarians, ordinary English speakers uncovered a whole new lot of problems: they found that 'he or she' and all its forms is simply too clumsy to use:

If anyone calls, please tell him or her that he or she is welcome to come on whichever evening he or she prefers.

Some writers who like things to be tidy deal with these problems by alternating between 'he' and 'she'. Others, in desperation (or defiance) have even made up new pronouns such as s/he, sher and shim. But what is wrong with saying 'they'? On the occasions when it's not the most elegant solution — now and then it can get tangled up with a real plural — you can convert its antecedent to a plural; use a singular pronoun; or throw the whole sentence out, go to bed and try again tomorrow.

The passive voice and the pursuit of vividness

Verbs can be used in either the active or passive voice. Your teachers probably told you about it at school — or maybe you were told about it at school:

They told you. (Active)
You were told. (Passive)

New writers are often told to avoid the passive on the grounds that it lacks vividness — that it doesn't present a sharp picture of someone doing something. But vividness should be pursued only when you want it; meaning is much more important than mere vividness. The passive voice is useful when, for whatever reason, you want to emphasise what was done rather than who did it: the difference between 'The butler has been murdered' (and now there's no one to serve the tea) and 'someone has murdered the butler' (and we'd better call M. Poirot).

The choice between active and passive has many advantages. It lets you leap past unimportant events; it allows you greater accuracy of meaning; it lets you arrange the word order so that a key word can fall where there is a natural stress, and so be emphasised.

Overuse of the passive is sometimes a problem with new writers. If you have trouble getting pictures out of your head and onto paper you can sometimes seize on the passive as a magic cloak to cover up the deficiency. This is all right with things that you can see, such as 'candles were brought' or 'socks were darned' or 'trees were felled'. Even if we don't see who is doing the bringing, the darning or the felling, we still have a shadowy picture of someone doing it. But verbs like 'enjoy', 'love' and 'dislike' can't be visualised so easily; they need someone to do the enjoying, the loving or disliking.

If you find yourself writing sentences like 'Picnics were enjoyed during the summer months' you should ask yourself exactly what you are trying to say. Emotion lies at the heart of good writing; but without a person to have the emotions, the writing will be empty.

Vivid words

Contrary to what many of us were told at school, you don't get vivid writing just by inserting vivid adjectives. You are more likely to get it by cutting out unnecessary words (especially unnecessary adjectives) and by finding specific words rather than general ones. For example:

'It was a lovely day. The coloured leaves were falling from the tree and the garden looked beautiful.' (Anon.)

Italo Calvino in *If on a Winter's Night a Traveller* did it much better:

'The ginkgo leaves fell like fine rain from the boughs and dotted the lawn with yellow.'

Before reaching automatically for words like tree, food, highly polished furniture, fruit, consider the possibilities of specific words like messmate, swamp mahogany, she-oak; baked potatoes, rye bread, cheese; rosewood table, mahogany chiffonier; apples, mangoes, plums and peaches.

If you are like most writers you will enjoy browsing through a dictionary or a thesaurus occasionally. One thing you shouldn't use a thesaurus for is finding synonyms for their own sake, simply to avoid using a word more than once. If a word is the right word, why shouldn't you use it as often as you need it? If the repetition seems inelegant, don't forget what pronouns are for.

Your foot in the door; the pluperfect tense

Most stories are told in the ordinary past tense — 'She was a teacher' — but occasionally you need to bring in a more distant past, one that existed before the story began, perhaps, and that is when you reach for the pluperfect tense — 'She had been a teacher'.

New writers sometimes develop an inordinate fondness for this tense, and can write several pages of it all in one go, as if the ordinary past tense had got lost somewhere and a substitute was needed. If you are a beginner and insecure, the pluperfect can feel reassuringly writerly and correct — after all, you see it all the time in published books. But that is probably because the pluperfect often introduces flashbacks:

> Julia had visited Beachworld once before. It was during the school holidays, and she went with her grandmother.

You'll notice that after that 'had visited' you probably won't need any more 'hads'. The pluperfect works like a door out of the story; through it you can glance out at an earlier past, or you can walk right out and explore it. Now and then you might need to use the pluperfect to remind readers of where they are, but what doesn't work is the constant use of the pluperfect with every verb:

> Julia remembered last night's supper. The tray had been loaded with delicacies of every kind: quails' eggs (Peter had collected them while the quails had been otherwise amused); stuffed peas (the under-chef had stuffed them while he had waited for the rose-petal aspic to set) . . .

Once again, you can see that ordinary, everyday spoken language works best. So if having a rule about language makes you feel better, here is one: *Always use the ordinary form if you can. If the sentence sounds funny, change it. If it sounds even funnier, change it back again.*

Language rules are constantly changing, but that doesn't mean we should throw the rules out and not have any at all; a language is a language and not a set of grunts precisely because it does have rules. As a custodian of the language you have an obligation to your young readers: you should understand the rules, what they do and why they exist, before you start throwing them away, and certainly before you invent new ones. That's why it's a good idea to look at dictionaries and style manuals occasionally. Language is an important tool, just as important as your experience, and this is a good way to sharpen it.

When you have checked a word or construction and found that it is frowned on, that doesn't mean you have to give it up. Language is changing all the time. If what you have written is clearer or easier or more familiar than the official correct form, go ahead and use it. Dictionaries and style manuals will catch up with you eventually.

6 WHAT IS A STORY?

One of the differences between a story and a chance collection of events is that a story has a point, a reason within itself for existing. Because stories are about people, the point is usually the main character's driving aim, and the story is the account of how the character achieves or fails to achieve it. As soon as the aim is achieved the tension dissipates, and with it our need to keep reading.

Imagine a story in which Brian's aim is to possess a magic bicycle. He asks his aunt (who is by way of being a witch) if she will give him one; she says yes, and produces it. But now what? That is where the story must finish — there is nothing left for Brian to do. You could write lots of scenes about Brian's magic bicycle and how it amazes people, but without the unifying thread that is Brian's aim, it won't be a real story with climax, resolution and ending; it will just be a collection of scenes about a magic bicycle.

Other characters in a story have aims too, and conflict between these aims adds interest and complexity to the story. It might be the aim of Brian's aunt not to let him have any sort of bicycle, let alone a magic one; or perhaps it is her aim to give him one, but allow him to keep it only if he fulfils certain conditions. Or perhaps it is another character's aim to seize the magic bicycle by trickery or by force. In all these cases there are possibilities for a story.

Another difference between chance events and a story is that a story has a pattern, letting us make guesses about what is going to happen. For children even more than for adults this chance to predict is an important part of reading. It's so important that if children can't discern a pattern — if they don't see that the clusters of events are leading somewhere — they will put the book down and watch television instead.

As they get older and gain experience in reading, children are able to recognise larger, more complex story-patterns. So while a child of six may need to see a pattern emerging in the first sentences, a ten-year-old may be willing to wait for a page, and a fifteen-year-old may be willing to wait for a chapter or more before a story-pattern appears.

The framework underlying this story-pattern is plot. In adult books the definition of 'plot' can be quite subtle and can include all sorts of new and interesting structures. It may even abandon story altogether. But to be accessible to children a book needs a plot in the traditional sense: the sort of framework that tells us what someone wanted and what they did to get it, and what the consequences were, in roughly that order.

Many experienced writers don't bother too much about plot in their first draft — they know from experience and from the feel of the story how it has to go. Less-experienced writers may feel they need a thread to guide them through the labyrinth. If so, one way of writing a children's story is to work out a brief story idea, and then fit it to an existing framework. Frameworks are easy to come by — if you pull apart a few jokes or folktales you will find plenty — but here are two straightforward ones that will keep you out of trouble.

The quest

In this sort of story the goal is reached over a number of episodes. These can be scenes, chapters or collections of chapters, depending on the length of the story. Quests are different from other sorts of plots in that the episodes don't have to build on one another; they are strung together like beads on a chain, and have a cumulative effect. Episodes can be completely self-contained, or linked in any way the author fancies — logically, thematically or poetically. E. Nesbit's *The Story of the Treasure Seekers*, Mem Fox's *Possum Magic*, and Russell Hoban's *The Mouse and his Child* and *How Tom Beat Captain Najork and his Hired Sportsmen* are all quests.

In quests, as in any other sort of story, the central character's goal needs to be something important — something that both you and your readers can believe in. The treasure seekers want to get their father back, along with their comfortable middle-class existence; Hush wants to become visible again (the story taps into the childhood fear of invisibility); the mouse's child wants a mother and a home; Tom wants the freedom to be a child.

Desires for family, home, love and security are all strong enough to make a story, but desires for a skateboard or even a magic bicycle could be less convincing; after all, a quest has to be worth braving all those dangers for. So a trivial goal is less likely to work unless it stands for a deeper one; for example, the goal of Hoban's mice to become self-winding stands for the deeper one of obtaining control over their lives.

Tension in a quest story is kept high mainly by expectation. We know the quest will almost certainly succeed, otherwise there would be no story, but we still expect the author to know more than we do; when the ending comes we like to be pleasantly surprised. As each possible solution is ruled out our interest grows — what is the answer? how will the wish be attained? — and when the surprise ending comes, we want to see not only an unexpected way of attaining the goal, but one which is still within the boundaries set by the story. (It's worth pointing out, perhaps, that the twists that make these satisfying surprises don't always appear at the planning stage; they are typical of write-and-see methods, see pages 42–3, in which the part of the story you have already written helps to generate what is still to come.)

Even though readers may be anxious about the outcome, story quests — at least for children — are in essence always successful. The goal attained might be different from the one we expected, but there will be a prize in the form of enlightenment, growth or understanding. To make the quest a complete waste of the character's time is to make it a complete waste of the reader's time too.

The classical five-act drama

Like the quest, you can use this framework for stories of all lengths, from picture books to long novels (and of course plays, where this framework originated). It's a refinement of the 'beginning, middle and end' that is so often recommended to new writers, but I think this version is more useful. The Greeks knew a thing or two about drama.

1 The pre-existing situation is shown to us, and we become aware of a change or disruption. The central character's goal becomes apparent.
2 'The plot thickens': associated problems may appear as other characters' goals conflict with those of the central character. There may be added complications — a time limit, perhaps, putting pressure on the central character to resolve the problems more quickly.
3 A solution is found. This could be the end of the story; but readers who understand the conventions of fiction are aware that the problem was solved too easily, and anyway, there is nearly half the book still to go. Sure enough, at the end of this section we discover that the solution doesn't work after all, and the situation is even worse than before.
4 Complications pile up. Worse fears are confirmed, disaster is imminent,

the situation seems hopeless. But in the background, clues dropped earlier have been working their way through the story, and now the main character, through intelligence, courage, perseverance, compassion, innocence or whatever human qualities you admire (with the probable exception of good luck), finally succeeds in achieving the goal, or a modified form of it.

5 This part is dedicated to the final unravelling of threads and the tying up of loose ends — though for the sake of credibility, one or two loose threads might deliberately be left dangling.

A defined framework is useful because that is what gives the story its shape, ensuring that you end up with a good, well-made animal with head, tail and body in functional proportion, and legs strong enough to hold it up.

If you are really unsure of yourself you can go about it this way: choose a length that is usual for the sort of book you propose (see the list on pages 104–6) and split your story into sections containing roughly the same number of words. This way you can make sure that everything works: that the opening phase of the story doesn't drag on, or that the climax doesn't come too early or too late.

But there can be a problem with following a predefined outline: you might be tempted to hang on to it even when the story no longer fits. When you are relaxed and working well the story will find its own complications, and they may differ from the ones you thought of. Failing to let your story develop naturally and logically is one of the quickest ways of killing it.

Another way of writing a story is to dispense with any sort of notes or outline and simply write; choose an opening sentence and see where it takes you. This method works very well if you are writing for adults, but in children's books it has a drawback: when you write this way you have less chance of coming across the tense, tightly structured sort of story that children need. The shorter the story, the less chance you have.

Within these two extremes there is a range of possible methods, the most favourable, I think, to be found at the write-and-see end of the spectrum. My own preference is to start with a character's name, a situation, a feeling and a setting, and a reasonable probable outcome. All the other aspects of the story — characters, plot, themes, subjects, twists in the plot, imagery — emerge by themselves out of the writing.

Writing a story this way — finding a logical outcome before you start writing — helps to reduce the number of stories that get lost or abandoned before you finish them. You probably know only too well the sort of thing that can happen: how, full of enthusiasm, you start off with characters and a situation, only to find a few paragraphs further on (or a few pages, or chapters, depending on the scale you are writing to) that your ideas are running out. You can't think what should happen next. You try sending the characters to various places where things might happen — to one another's houses, to football matches, to school, to a film — but they just stroll round in circles chatting to one another, and nothing happens. Nothing moves, nothing develops, and eventually the story shrivels and dies.

If in the beginning the story had had an end event that you could aim at, the intervening scenes would have had a purpose, and there would have been far less chance of getting stuck or running off the rails. You would at least have known what direction you should be heading in, and what events had to take place along the way.

Another way to start constructing a story is to choose a name, give the character a goal that you feel you could share, and consider the possible outcomes. Like this:

It's Henriette's first time at a writer's camp, and she doesn't like it; the only person she knows there is her friend Zoe, and Zoe doesn't like it either. It is the children's goal to get home again as soon as possible.

What could some of the possible outcomes be? The children might be successful and find a way of getting home immediately; or after a few days (but still well before the camp finishes); or only at the end of the camp when everyone else is going home too. Or they might be unsuccessful and have to stay to the end of the camp (but discover in the meantime that it is really fun). Any one of the outcomes I have suggested (and there are plenty more you could think of) would make a story, depending on the circumstances surrounding it. For example, what are Henriette and Zoe like? What is the camp like — is it just an ordinary camp, or is it as bad as the children think it is? Which outcome interests you most?

Your answers to these questions will help you decide what sort of plot the story will have — the two given in this chapter are by no means the only ones possible. Or if you are not going to bother with a plot, the outcome will tell you what sort of story it will be and how you might tackle it.

I WHO TELLS THE STORY?

Although the author decides what the characters will say and do and what will happen, the author of a story is not the narrator. The narrator, like a character in the story, is a persona invented for the purpose; a facet of the author's personality through which the story is filtered.

The narrator can be a main character in the story, or a peripheral one, or someone who stands right outside it. The one you choose will be a particular sort of person with a particular way of speaking, and will tell the story in their own way. That is why the opening sentence of a story is so important; not because it has to grab the reader's attention, as new writers are so often told, but because it has to grab the writer's attention. As you flick through opening sentences in your head, looking for the one that feels just right, you are actually auditioning different personae for the role of narrator.

At the very beginning of a story there are two questions to be answered: whose story it is, and who is going to tell it. That doesn't mean you must put off writing until you know the answers to these questions, although some writers prefer to work that way. It does mean that you may need to have more than one try before you decide.

Think of all the different stories that are buried in *Cinderella*. Apart from the story of Cinderella herself there is the stepmother's story, the elder or younger sister's story, the father's, or the prince's. You can tell the story as it happens, or shortly after the wedding, or when Cinderella and the prince are old and the story is a long way behind them.

Not all these stories will be equally interesting to you. The father's version will have a gap in it that will need to be filled in somehow, and the queen's version might be a different story entirely.

Once you have decided whose version of the story will be told, you still have to decide who will tell it. The story can be told by a character who takes part in the action, for example by Cinderella or the fairy godmother, or by someone standing outside it, such as Baron von Adel who lives in the neighbouring castle and who heard it from his seneschal; or it can be told by a self-effacing story-teller about whom we know nothing at all.

Each narrator, as well as having a different voice, will choose a particular viewpoint from which to tell the story. There are no rules — you can put the narrator anywhere you like. If you want the narrator to stand perfectly still, or to stay with one character, or to move about, shining a torch here and there; or if you want no narrator at all, and prefer to tell your story through letters, journals, diary extracts and old labels, the decision is yours. To help you choose, here are some of the many viewpoints that are possible.

Universal viewpoints

Universal viewpoints are big brushes for painting broad sweeps; universal narrators can range widely over a story-landscape, lighting up details here and there and moving on when necessary. There are two kinds.

Objective narrators

An objective narrator can choose any part of the broad picture, observing characters and recording what they do and say, but without looking into people's minds. So in this story-telling mode there is no one to tell us what the characters are thinking; often we don't even know what the narrator is thinking.

Objective narrators were used a lot in the nineteenth century; you probably remember Victorian novels in which characters became greatly agitated, blushed, trembled, tottered, turned pale and swooned when something dramatic happened to them. Now we consider such reactions overdone but the objective narrator still has a place, especially at the beginnings of novels.

> On a hot afternoon in December, two young men with sunburnt complexions might have been observed walking along a narrow sandy track, known to the locals as Old Man's Track, on their way to Surfer's Beach.
> Each carried a surfboard under one arm, and each carried a towel slung round his neck. They were deep in conversation, and as they talked they moved their free arms in a constant to-and-fro motion across their faces, as if gesticulating in the eagerness of their discourse . . .

This narrator is sticking very closely to the observed facts, not even telling us if the young men had been seen by anyone else or not. We aren't even told why they were moving their arms; we are left to guess whether they were arguing heatedly or just brushing away flies.

The objective narrator is often used in picture books, especially those with a very short text, where a clean and uncluttered treatment is needed.

Omniscient narrators

If an author prefers to let readers know more clearly what is in the characters' minds, there is the omniscient narrator. This narrator, like God, knows everything, can go anywhere, can see into all the characters' minds at once and tell us what is there.

If there is such a thing as a 'natural' story-telling mode, this is it. This is the viewpoint of once upon a time, and the one that new writers seem to reach for first; perhaps because it is so obvious, or perhaps because it was the first one they ever heard — not only folk stories, but many stories for small children are told by this narrator.

> There was a man, and he was very greedy. Whenever he saw his neighbour with anything of value he used to think, I must have that. And he used to plan and scheme until he got it. In this way he became very rich.
>
> One day his neighbour, who in this way had become very poor, said 'I must teach this greedy neighbour of mine a lesson.'

As you see, the omniscient story-teller knows the contents of all the characters' minds, and the story can move ahead swiftly.

You might wonder why anyone would use any other viewpoint if the omniscient narrator does the job so well. Part of the reason is that this viewpoint is not always as flexible as it seems.

One difficulty is that the omniscient narrator needs to be impartial, if the narrative is not to be skewed or confused. If there are many characters you can find that the narrator seems to be standing a long way off; there is a curiously remote feeling in the narrative. This isn't necessarily wrong — it might be just the effect you are after — but if it is unintentional it may keep readers out of the story.

Handling this omniscient narrative style can call for a great deal of skill; characters need to be drawn with care, or the long view may make them difficult to tell apart.

The omniscient narrator is not necessarily the best viewpoint for every story. It may not work so well in stories that depend on a mystery; if the narrator knows everything, it may be difficult to conceal facts from the reader and remain credible. (But if you are determined, it can be done.)

Yet another difficulty can come from the omniscient narrator knowing as much as the author: authors occasionally forget they have delegated the job to a narrator and intrude into the story themselves:

'Come on then,' said Dad, and they all piled into the car. Jamie got into the back and did his seat belt up at once because safety is very important.

This sort of intrusion is nearly always unwelcome and it can happen with any kind of viewpoint, but it is most common in universal ones.

Limited viewpoints

With a limited viewpoint the story is told from the point of view of one person. The narrator climbs into one character's head (usually the central character's but not necessarily) and the story comes to us filtered through that character's perception.

First person

Unless we are given clues to the contrary, first-person narrative often carries with it an extra air of truth; even though we know the author is not speaking directly to us, we still half believe they might be. Do you remember when you were a child, how disappointed you were when you discovered that the 'I' of a story wasn't really its author?

Because of this air of truth, the first-person narrator is often favoured for fantasy stories. There is also a bonus: the narrator, observing the setting with the limited view of a child, is not expected to know any more about it than a child would — something that can save the author a lot of work.

Another advantage is that, since the first-person narrator addresses us directly, the set-up details — those things we need to know before the story can begin — can be explained to us directly, as in a letter to a friend. Look at this:

My name's Trogh. The planet where I live has two suns, and at the proper times you can see the two shadows crossing. We call it suncross, and it's an important time for silence and prayer, and for making up quarrels. Each person takes a special twin-lensed lamp and goes on their suncross rounds, visiting people they might have offended since last suncross. Sometimes people meet on the way to visit each other, and that is considered very good luck.

It's certainly not exciting, but it gets by; all the first-person narrator has to do is address us directly. Without the voice of a professional story-teller to come between us, we are willing to believe Trogh's story, for the time being at least.

But look at the same passage told in the third person:

The planet where Trogh lived had two suns, and at the proper times you could see the two shadows crossing. Trogh's people called it suncross, and it was an important time for silence and prayer, and for making up quarrels. Each person used to take a special twin-lensed lamp and go on their suncross rounds, visiting people they might have offended since last suncross. Sometimes people met on the way to visit each other, and that was considered very good luck.

It's boring, and the longer it goes on the more boring it gets.

But the first-person narrator has shortcomings too. The most obvious one is that the narrator's knowledge is limited to what the 'I' knows. Gretel can't tell us what the witch had for breakfast because she wasn't there; Cinderella's stepmother can't tell us what the fairy godmother looked like because they have never met, and so on. There is something wrong with this, for example:

I sat down to watch the film. Behind me some people were whispering too quietly for me to hear.

'What do you think of the film?' said one.

This limitation can make it difficult to tell your reader things the narrating character doesn't know — that someone is sneaking up behind them, for example — but there are ways round the problem. You can give your narrating character clues, and let them be a little less smart than your readers; or if you have a bigger slab of information to get across you can try letters, notes and diaries; or you can let another character relate what they have seen. But keep these devices within bounds, perhaps cutting back to the 'I' of the story from time to time. If children are kept too long from the narrating character they will simply skip ahead to where it reappears.

I should also mention another difficulty with first-person narrative, one that is peculiar to children's fiction. There is a convention in adult fiction that the first-person narrator is literate, articulate and observant, and can bring to the job the same degree of sensitivity and insight as a third-person narrator. In children's fiction this convention doesn't exist. The first-person narrator in children's fiction is nearly always a child, and speaks with the appropriate voice. Immediately you accept this idea you limit the narrator's opportunities, and you risk losing any chance of wisdom, insight, poetic vision or elegant language that might have been expected from an adult narrator. That is why first-person narrative in children's fiction is so beguilingly easy to write, and so difficult to write well. You need subtlety, skill and cunning to conceal in the child's voice what the adult needs to say.

But it is possible, as these examples (from Nigel and Caron Krauth's *I Thought You Kissed With Your Lips*) show:

> '"Virginal" was a word that kind of trapped you between what you were and what you wanted to be. You wanted to be free of it, but at the same time you weren't at all sure what being free of it meant.'

And also:

> 'I looked around at her. Madge was right. That was exactly what I felt about fourteen-year-old — not just time but — everything. Everything was much too precious, too vulnerable, too easily lost or cracked or broken. I felt like I was living in a glass bowl. I could see the things I wanted, but couldn't touch them. If I moved too quickly or too wildly, the bowl would break . . . and what would be the consequences? Freedom or disaster?'

Second person

There is such a thing as second-person narrative. I mention it for the sake of completeness; in children's books you don't see it often outside choose-your-own-adventure books, but plenty of adult writers have used it in more challenging ways. You might have seen something like this:

> You wake one morning to discover that someone has boarded up your window and taken your bed away. Your room is completely dark, and you are lying on what seems to be a pile of old socks. You wish you had taken them to the laundromat when you had the chance.

Third person

This is where you perform the magic trick of jumping into someone else's skin — seeing the world through their eyes and hearing it through their ears — with the added complexity of having a narrator along for the ride.

In this viewpoint, you stay in the head of one character for long sections of narrative or throughout the whole story, and the reader's experience of the story is limited to that character's thoughts and perceptions. In this scene from L. M. Boston's *The Children of Green Knowe*, where Toseland visits his great-grandmother, all the narrator's observations come to us filtered through Toseland:

> 'The room seemed to be the ground floor of a castle, much like the ruined castles that he had explored on school picnics, only this was not a ruin. It looked as if it never possibly could be. Its thick stone walls were strong, warm and lively. It was furnished with comfortable old-fashioned things as though living in castles was quite ordinary. Toseland stood just inside the door and felt it must be a dream.
>
> His great-grandmother was sitting by a huge open fireplace where logs and peat were burning. The room smelled of woods and wood-smoke. He forgot about her being frighteningly old. She had short silver curls and her face had so many wrinkles it looked as if someone had been trying to draw her for a very long time and every line put in had made the face more like her. She was wearing a soft dress of folded velvet that was as black as a hole in darkness. The room was full of candles in glass candlesticks, and there was candlelight in her ring when she held out her hand to him.'

Once you become aware of limited third-person narrative and get used to writing in it, you will find that you can handle other viewpoints too. Your story-telling will become much more assured, and you will also notice a difference in the way you think about story material; you might find that a story idea that seemed sterile before is now alive with possibilities. In many ways, the viewpoint determines the story.

One of the biggest difficulties that new writers have with limited third-person narrative is maintaining it: it is very easy to slip out of it and into the mode of the omniscient narrator. In fact, it's so easy to do that new writers are sometimes told that they must never do it.

This rule, too, can be broken. If there is a rule in story-telling it's this: The Story Comes First. That is, the story is more important than any techniques for telling it. If the best way of telling a limited-viewpoint story demands a break in viewpoint, do it. It is only the accidental, jarring breaks in viewpoint that you must avoid. Like this one:

> Imogen walked into the crowded hall, searching for the man who had treated her so kindly, wondering if she would ever see him again. She scanned every face in the crowd, looking for the one with the bushy white whiskers and the jolly red nose, and then she saw him standing in a corner.
>
> 'Santa!' she said, appearing at his elbow.

The word 'appearing' jars; we are seeing things from Imogen's point of view, so when we are told that she has appeared we imagine for a moment that she has materialised there. Instead, we are meant to understand that it is Father Christmas who sees her appearing; without warning, the viewpoint has shifted to him.

One or two examples like this in a story might go unnoticed if you are lucky. If when you read your finished story, you notice it has a hazy, unfocused air, or if the main character seems to be coming across as a minor one, don't immediately start poking in adjectives and adverbs, or redrawing the character. The problem could be accidental shifts in viewpoint.

Third-person limited viewpoint shares at least one difficulty with first-person. A story-teller who is limited to Cinderella's point of view can't tell us what the prince had for dinner last night because Cinderella doesn't know it. For the same reason the story-teller probably can't tell us about Prince Charming's childhood, or what he is thinking at the moment.

The solutions are similar to those in first-person narrative, and here too it is a good idea to be careful; all of them involve interrupting the story to some extent. If you are writing a longer novel — say for fourteen-year-olds and up — you will get away with it more easily, but younger children are likely to skip these interpolated bits and go looking for the main character again.

There is no 'correct' viewpoint for any story. There is just the viewpoint, or viewpoints, that best suit you, your story and the narrator you want to use.

As I said earlier, when people start writing they usually choose the omniscient narrator first. If this is the narrator you have been using till now, perhaps it's time to branch out a little.

8 DIALOGUE

The amount of dialogue you put in your story is up to you. Some writers like to use a lot, others like to use it just to highlight a point. It doesn't matter which you prefer, but you should be aware that dialogue is not a good narrative tool. It's limited by the vocabulary, speech rhythms, understanding and personality of the character who is speaking.

It's true that plays consist almost entirely of dialogue, but the dialogue of a play is interpreted by a team of people — director, designers, and above all, highly skilled actors who work hard at unpicking the meaning from the bare dialogue before passing it on to an audience. A reader has only the written dialogue, with, perhaps, a stage direction or two in the form of an adverb, as in 'she whispered gratefully'. Good writers of fiction, like good playwrights, keep these directions to a minimum; wherever possible they let the dialogue itself suggest how it should be spoken.

Often, the dialogue will also tell us who is speaking, but for the sake of clarity sometimes you will need to use an attribution — a label in the form of 'she said' or 'Mr Corcoran said'. You can put attributions either before or after the speech, but if they come first, the trend is towards no punctuation: He said 'I hope you can come'. But some editors still prefer a comma: She said, 'It's too cold'.

If there is an attribution at the end of the speech, you end the speech with a comma, question mark or exclamation mark, but never with a full stop; and the attribution begins with a small letter (except for proper nouns, of course):

'It's raining,' the postman said.
'It's snowing!' his wife said.
'Is it?' he said.
'I just told you it was!' she said.

If you like, you can invert subject and verb and say 'said the postman' instead of 'the postman said'. But you can only use this inversion at the end of a speech. Putting it at the beginning (Said the postman 'The Page Three Girl made me do it') is considered a mortal sin.

If you write for older children over, say, nine, and prefer to avoid attributions, there are several ways of doing it. You can drop in a name here and there:

'I'll fix that, Julian!'

Only don't overdo it, unless you want your character to sound like a used-car dealer. In real life people don't use other people's names a great deal, and we become suspicious when they do; we suspect they are trying to sell us something — a car, a time-share unit, or even a religion.

The way dialogue is set out also helps to let readers know who is speaking. The convention is that you start a new paragraph for each new speaker, no matter how short the speech:

'Did you hear that?'
'What?'
'That.'

But if a speaker is interrupted by narrative and then continues, you stay in the same paragraph:

'Wait!' said Henry, signalling her to stop. 'Did you hear that?'
'I hope,' said Abigail, peering out of the window, 'that the roof doesn't leak.'

You'll notice that full stops occur in their usual places — at the end of sentences — and if there is no full stop, the speech continues with a small letter.

If a speech needs to be broken up into more than one paragraph, the convention (so that we know it is still the same person speaking) is to repeat the opening quotation marks at the beginning of the new paragraph, without closing them in the paragraph before. Like this:

'And that,' said Professor Lincoln, 'concludes my comments on the moons of Jupiter.
'The rings of Saturn, however . . .'

What actors call business (meaning 'busy-ness' or activity) can reveal who the speaker is, if you put both business and speech in the same paragraph:

Alison gazed into the cat's eyes. 'They're like oranges.'

It is fortunately going out of fashion, but some writers of stories for younger children still worry about the constantly repeated 'saids' and vary them with verbs like laughed, agreed, opined, stated, sniffed, gurgled, chuckled, chortled, whistled and so on. Alternatives like this draw even more attention to themselves than the humble 'said'; unless the replacement verb really is a way of saying something — like 'whispered', 'mumbled', 'murmured' or 'shouted' — you are probably better off sticking to 'said'. Go carefully with words like 'exclaimed' and 'laughed'. They are ways of making a noise, but not necessarily of saying anything; and although they are used a lot in attributions they sound very old-fashioned. I prefer 'exclaim' and 'laugh' for exclaiming and laughing, and 'say' for saying.

The real problem with repeating 'said' is not so much the repetition but the monotonous rhythm; in short lines of dialogue the attributions tend to fall directly on top of one another, like badly-laid bricks:

'Josie, are you coming?' Joel said.
　'In a minute,' Josie said.
　'Hurry, we'll miss the bus,' he said.

There are several ways of fixing this. You can break up the knocking rhythm by staggering some of the attributions. So you might break up a line and put the attribution in the middle, or put it at the beginning of the line instead of the end. You can also manipulate the rhythm by using names instead of pronouns now and then. Like this:

Joel said 'Josie, are you coming?'
　'In a minute,' said Josie.
　'Hurry,' said Joel. 'We'll miss the bus.'

As you see, once the rhythm is broken up the 'saids' tend to disappear.

No matter how old or young your readers are, any business you include needs to be carefully observed, and relevant to the character and the situation. In this way business can be a valuable addition to the story. For example, you can let us know that there is a difference between a character's inner state and what they are telling us:

Henry turned away, folding his arms across his chest. 'I told you. I'm perfectly happy.'

Business can also move the story along, or draw attention to symbols and images that you want to keep near the surface:

Abigail drew a pentacle in the sand with her toe and rubbed it out again. 'No problems. I'll wait for you here.'

One thing you shouldn't do is reach for any old bit of business just for the sake of avoiding a 'said' — or rather, you should think twice before keeping it. Take particular care with actions that are commonplace — people running their fingers through their hair, blowing hair out of their eyes, biting their lip, sitting down or standing up. It's true that in the real world people do these things hundreds of times a day. They also say 'Um' and 'Ah' a lot, wander from the point, or forget what they were talking about and start again, but you don't put all these lapses in the dialogue. A piece of fiction is not a faithfully copied piece of real life, it is a crafted impression of an unreal narrator's impression of real life. There is a lot of difference.

Dialogue works best if you can make it do more than one job. If, as well as telling us what is said, the dialogue and its associated narrative advances the story, tells us how it is said and by whom, and what kind of person the speaker is, you are probably winning.

The easiest way to tell us how dialogue is spoken (perhaps too easy) is to slip an adverb after the verb:

'I haven't done my homework,' Fiona said miserably.

Miss Featherstone stared at her coldly. 'I shall speak to you later,' she said sternly.

As you can see, the first adverb, 'miserably', is doing a reasonable job — if you cut it out you also damage the sense (though a piece of business would repair it, and so would more specific dialogue). You could make a case for 'coldly' for the same reason, but only just; people don't usually stare warmly. But 'sternly' should definitely go — it is obvious from the context how the words were said. In any case, three adverbs in a row are too many. A piece of writing in which there is scarcely a verb without an adverb tacked onto it becomes difficult and tiresome to read.

Writers for older children can avoid the problem altogether by choosing a more precise verb in the first place. But if you write stories for children under ten, your stock of usable verbs is smaller, and there's more chance that you'll need to use an adverb now and then. But take care; avoid using them to reinforce what we already know, or should have guessed:

'I hate you!' Margaret said angrily.

'There, there,' said Alice placatingly.

You can control how dialogue is to be read in more subtle ways by using rhythm, or more specifically the pauses. Inserting an attribution creates the effect of a pause in the words; and wherever there is a pause in the words, as if by magic a stress appears just before it. In the following examples you can see how varying the pauses varies the stress, giving a different shade of meaning to the words in each case:

'I,' said Miss Corcoran, 'believe that Harry is lying.' (And I don't care what the rest of you think.)

'I believe,' said Miss Corcoran, 'that Harry is lying.' (But I could be wrong.)

'I believe that Harry,' said Miss Corcoran, 'is lying.' (But the others may be telling the truth.)

My father was also fond of invoking Chekhov, and his advice to writers, 'Don't tell, show', also applies to characters and their dialogue. Consider all the ways of saying 'What did you say?' that different people might use. Pardon? Eh? What? I beg your pardon? Speak up, young man! These are not interchangeable ways of saying the same thing. They are all used by different kinds of people. A character's choice of words should go some way to revealing who that character is. This is why, when you want to convey what was said, you normally choose direct speech ('I'll come,') rather than indirect speech ('he said he would come') — unless the speech was so unimportant that you want to skate over it. In this case you might be able to leave it out entirely.

Direct speech:

'Are you coming to the Festival?' I asked.
  'All right then,' he said.

Indirect speech:

I asked if he was coming to the Festival and he said that he was.

(If you are tempted to say 'I asked if he *were* coming' see Chapter 5.)

Like distant viewpoints, a lot of indirect speech all at once can also make you feel as if you are looking through the wrong end of the telescope, and for the same reason: it is as if the narrator is too far away to hear, and can give us only the gist of what is said. It can be hard to enter a scene that has been written this way, which might explain the almost superstitious veneration that some beginning writers have for dialogue.

Some people seem to have an ear for dialogue; they notice idiosyncrasies in people's speech in the same way that other people notice nuances of colour or sound. If you are gifted in this way you are lucky. Not all good writers are good at dialogue.

If you suspect that dialogue may not be one of your strong points, there are several things you can do to improve it, or even to hide the fact. One way is to make the lines of dialogue very short; the shorter a speech is, the less chance for it to go wrong. Another way is to make sure that the lines of dialogue aren't interchangeable — try to see that all speakers have their own voice. If in doubt, test suspect lines, if the sense allows, by giving them to other speakers. Do the words sound best with the speaker they are written for? Even if you have followed the first suggestion and your dialogue is terse to the point of being stylised, this should still work.

To give yourself some practice in creating a character's voice, try retelling all or some of *Cinderella* in the voice of the prince's mother, Cinderella's father, or Cinderella's stepmother. To practise creating a character as well, don't be afraid to let your characters bend the story their way. Narrators don't always have to tell the truth.

Like other aspects of writing, dialogue is an illusion. If you took the trouble to record the conversation in a coffee shop or a bar, you would hear speech full of trivia, hesitancies, corrections, indistinct words and meaningless expressions. In conversation, a speaker has tone of voice, gesture and expression to help convey meaning, but the main difference is in the purpose; ordinary conversation is intended to communicate ideas from one speaker to another.

Written dialogue has much more to do. It has to reveal character and relationships, create ironies, reveal situations, establish or maintain mood, reveal states of mind (including those that a character is hiding), keep threads or motifs running, reinforce themes, regulate pace and advance the plot.

Different writers use dialogue in different ways, but it's a mistake, whatever the length of the book, to let characters sit around talking, doing nothing more than creating the mood of people sitting around talking. If you have an ear for dialogue you will have to be strict with yourself and cut out idle exchanges.

Dialogue, even when it is being used to advance the plot, tends to slow the action wherever it occurs. This can be quite useful at high points and low points of the narrative, where you might want a controlled pause. But if the pause is uncontrolled and the dialogue just trickles on, the story's impetus will trickle away with it.

If you are a fluent writer of dialogue you might be misled into imagining that it's just a matter of letting it flow — thinking yourself into the characters and letting them say what people in those circumstances would say. Writing in this way produces, without effort, copious amounts of dialogue that is barely distinguishable from real life. But it's not real life you're writing, it's fiction. And fiction needs to be shaped.

Even if you do find dialogue easy (particularly if you find it easy!) it's a good idea to decide beforehand what you want it to convey. Then, from the range of things a character could say, you choose the words that do the job best — the words that do several jobs instead of just one or two.

Let's say you are coming to the end of a scene between Theo and Elisa, who have been spending a day at the beach. The scene actually ends with a piece of narrative, but you decide that a bit of dialogue after that will provide a satisfying cadence. Almost any line will do this simple job, and this is why dull dialogue often creeps in at the ends of scenes:

> Purple shadows were stretching across the beach as they picked their way
> through the dunes towards home.
> 'What a fantastic day,' said Elisa.
> 'Yes it was,' said Theo.

Because of their position at the end of the scene, these lines of dialogue have a weightiness out of all proportion to their meaning. But just because you can occasionally get away with dialogue like this doesn't mean you should; there is nothing to stop you trying for something more interesting.

Rendering accents

Whether it's a German accent or Italian or Irish or bevan-bogan, if you aren't personally acquainted with the voice or the language you risk making some horrible mistakes. Dialect words don't always mean what you think they do; Germans don't always put the verb at the end of the sentence; people from poorer families don't always mispronounce words. If you get fundamentals like this wrong you can bet that some of your readers will notice, and for them the book may be spoilt.

A more tactful way of reproducing accents — a way that is more respectful towards your characters — is to reproduce just the flavour. Subtle manipulation of speech rhythms, careful choice of language and an occasional idiosyncrasy will do a better job than phonetic reproduction, and will also be kinder to your readers. For example, who could possibly mistake the accent behind these words, spoken by Grandma in Katherine Paterson's *Come Sing, Jimmy Jo*?

> '"Just a purty song's why I cry. You know that, boy. A song like that's pure
> delight. And Lord, boy, you sing it like a angel."'

9 STORY BEGINNINGS

Here is something to sharpen your teeth on. What do you think of the following passage as the opening to a story? Do you think it works? If so, why? And if not, why not?

> The boy ran swiftly, his bare feet thudding over the hard ground, his breath escaping in hoarse rasps, a cloud of dust swirling at his heels. From time to time he stopped, head cocked to one side, as if listening; then on he sped across the narrow plateau. Behind him could be heard the sounds of pursuit: the shouts and cries of an enraged mob.
>
> At the top of the cliff the boy paused, then plunged down a rocky path into the ravine. At the bottom of the ravine he stopped once more, panting, then suddenly doubled back, apparently in the hope of escaping his pursuers.
>
> Then as he reached a rockfall that partially blocked the ravine, one of the larger rocks moved. The boy took a step back, flinging his arms up to protect himself. It was a dragon!

Put your answer aside. We'll look at it later on.

Alice, wanting to know where to begin her story, was told 'Begin at the beginning and go on till you come to the end, then stop'. It sounds like good advice, but for writers there is a flaw: just how do you know where the beginning is? And is it the best beginning?

Even if you are the kind of writer who just sits down and writes and makes sense of it later, rather than the kind of writer who ponders and makes sense of it before, there are two things about a story that you will need to decide: where it begins, and how you will go about beginning it. Will your summer holiday story begin when the family book the campsite? When they start packing? When they arrive? Or after they have been holidaying for a week? And how will you go about establishing the background details? Will you explain them at the outset, or plunge straight into the story and weave them in as you go? Both approaches are possible.

Starting outside the story

By far the easiest way to establish background details is to start the story with them, dumping them in the reader's lap all in one go:

> The Wallace children were to leave for their holiday at the end of September. However, this year the children would not be holidaying with their parents — instead the two Doctors Wallace would be going to a pediatrics conference in Hong Kong. So the five children, Roberta, 13, Mark, 11, Vanessa, 9, Harry, 7, and Pickle, 5, would be looked after by their aunt Hadie, whom they had not seen for six years.

But as you can see, it's also very dull; we want to get into the story, not just be told about it.

Starting with a scene

Because it's so important to get into the story quickly, many writers prefer to skip these introductory explanations and go straight to the first scene. If the story is to be told by a limited third-person narrator, there might be one sentence from an objective narrator to start it off:

> It was raining at Basset Beach. If you sat in the cottage and looked out, beyond the curtains of rain could be seen the grey sand of the beach, and behind that the darker grey of rocks, sea and sky.

But there is no need to start with the objective narrator. You can just as easily start in Roberta's head:

> Roberta wiped condensation from the window and stared out at the monochrome landscape. Beyond the curtains of rain she could see the dark grey of the beach, and behind that the darker greys of rocks, sea and sky.

As well as the other differences between the two versions, you'll notice that this narrator has a more subjective view of Roberta, thinking of her as 'Roberta' rather than 'Roberta Wallace'.

Starting with a scene gets into the story faster, but it's more difficult than dumping everything in the reader's lap; now you have to make the scene work in its own right while at the same time filling in the background. It needs a lot of care; if you put too much information into the scene you will muddy the story for us, and if you don't put in enough we won't know what is going on.

Starting with dialogue

This is even more important when you consider a third, even faster approach, in which you go one step further and start in the middle of the scene with a line of dialogue:

> 'It's never going to stop raining, never!' Roberta wiped a patch of fog from the window and peered out at the monochrome landscape. 'Look at that rain — we'll be stuck in this cottage for ever and ever. Our holiday'll be ruined!'

But probably more bad books have been written with this kind of opening than with any other; it's not easy to do well. The trouble is that as soon as your character has delivered that opening line, you are back where you started. You still have to reveal the background details and keep the story moving, but now you also have to let the reader know who is speaking, and to whom. It's a juggling act that is easy to muff; you probably remember books in which you had to read the beginning several times before you knew what was going on.

Even if you do manage to keep all the balls in the air, you can still find your characters just sitting round chatting, leaving you to drag in the luggage:

> 'It's never going to stop raining, never!' Roberta wiped a patch of fog from the window and peered out at the monochrome landscape. 'Look at that rain — we'll be stuck in this cottage for ever and ever. Our holiday'll be ruined!'
>
> 'Don't say that,' said Aunt Hadie. 'Your parents wouldn't like to think you weren't enjoying yourselves.'
>
> Mark looked up from his book. 'While they're sunning themselves in Hong Kong, you mean?'
>
> 'Sunning themselves?' said Roberta. 'It rains all the time in Hong Kong. They have typhoons there.'
>
> 'What's a typhoon?' asked Harry.
>
> 'It's something doctors get,' said Pickle, 'when they go to conferences.'

And so on. It looks harmless enough, and it does bring in a little background, but it doesn't do enough of the things good dialogue should do. Worse, it seems to have no connection with any story that might follow.

Because children's books are so short, there is no room for an opening section that bears no relation to the story. The opening section needs to contain the seeds of the story itself; not only the characters and the setting, but the story's underlying ideas — relationships, motifs and themes — all need to be established at the outset as neatly and as elegantly as possible.

You'll notice that the first kind of opening — the one that starts outside the story — has a different feel to it from the second one. The narrator's voice sounds more distant, more impartial when we are outside the story, and becomes warmer and more subjective as we move into it. This shift doesn't trouble us when we move from the outside to the inside, but when the shift goes the other way there is often a jolt; we feel as if the narrator has grabbed us by the lapel and is dragging us away from the story:

'It's never going to stop raining, never!' Roberta wiped a patch of fog from the window and peered out at the monochrome landscape. 'We'll be stuck in this cottage for ever. Our holiday'll be ruined!'

The Wallace children and their aunt had been holidaying at Basset Beach for a whole week now, and so far it had rained every day. Roberta was disappointed; she was a keen swimmer and she had been looking forward to teaching her youngest sister how to swim.

See what I mean? Once you have entered the viewpoint character's head it is too late to give us information in this way. You can get away with a sentence or two — the reader will assume we are still in the character's head; but once it becomes clear that the narrator is outside the story again, our interest fades. (This doesn't apply to first-person narrative, of course, where the narrator and the viewpoint character are the same person.)

Starting in the middle

A story implies some change or deviation from existing events, and a common place to start a story is just before this change occurs. But if your story situation is one that needs a great deal of explaining you might need to start further back; usually, the more explaining you have to do the further back in the story you will need to start, just to give yourself room to weave it all in.

If there is a great deal of information to be conveyed you might find yourself pushing the story so far back that the lack of action becomes a problem. If the real story begins when a person who is on holiday meets someone, it is usually not a good idea to clog the beginning with long scenes of people planning their holiday, or packing, or fighting in the car on the way there.

One way round the difficulty is to start not further back but further *into* the story — at any dramatic event that suits you — and then fill in the events leading up to it. This has the effect of adding forward motion, and therefore tension, to the story. The author has lit the firecracker, and now the reader must wait for the bang.

No matter how you begin your story, background establishment detail needs to be carefully masked; don't let your readers become aware of the machinery working underneath. You should bring in the details gradually, embedding them so firmly in the story that readers can't tell the difference between explanation and story; and if you do this so skilfully that no one notices how skilful you have been, you have done a competent job.

Rough beginnings

There can be two quite different beginnings to a story: the rough beginning a writer sets down just so as to get started, and the beginning the polished story eventually gets. There is no rule that says they must be different; it seems to depend on the kind of writer you are. Some writers prefer to work their way into a new story and start by writing down whatever comes to mind. Later on they may decide to change the opening, or even toss out the whole of the first chapter. Other writers (I am one) get their opening sentence fixed and start from there.

A problem can arise when, taking Cobbett's advice, you just sit down and write what you think. If writing is indeed an attempt to discover meaning you may not know what the meaning is until later in the book, or even until you have got to the end of it. So the beginning of your first draft is likely to be full of unnecessary clutter — scenes that worked well at the time, but which now bear no relevance to the work as a whole. However much you like these scenes, you will have to be rigorous; no story should contain completely irrelevant material, certainly not children's stories and least of all in the beginning.

Now let's look at the start of this chapter again. The example of the story beginning was written from a universal viewpoint, that of the objective narrator, and you probably recognised the wrong-end-of-the-telescope effect; the narrator is so far away we don't even know the boy's name. Because of this we are mildly curious while we read the first few sentences, but when we get to the dragon our attention falters.

If you doubt that this is so, try putting a boy's name in place of 'the boy', and change the narrative voice from objective to subjective; that is, change 'could be heard' to 'he could hear' and delete 'as if' and 'apparently', then replace some of the objective observations with subjective ones. Now what do you think?

You are probably way ahead of me, but I'll ram my point home and repeat: good stories are about people. Chases or even dragons have no value as story material unless they are about someone. In the example I gave you, the boy has no name, we are given no insight into him, and so when he is confronted by a dragon we don't mind very much if it eats him.

There is a standard piece of advice offered to beginning writers: *Your opening sentence must grab the reader*. Oddly enough, this advice is offered by readers and teachers more often than by writers themselves (except perhaps journalists, but that's a different matter). Fiction writers know better than to offer advice like that; at the beginning of a new story the last thing a good writer should be thinking about is how to impress the reader. (If you don't believe me, browse through *It was a Dark and Stormy Night* — a collection of inspired, excruciatingly bad openings based on the principle of impressing the reader.)

The opening sentence is important, of course, but at this stage it's important to you, the writer, not to the reader. It's important to you because the opening sentence sets certain parameters: who the narrator is; whether they are male, female, young, or old — and whether they are inside the story or outside it, or completely invisible. As we've seen, a narrator can stand close to the events, or so far away that we seem to see everything through the wrong end of a telescope; or at any distance in between.

Just as you knew when you chose a character's name that you had got it right, you know when you have the right opening sentence. There is nothing mysterious about it. The right one just feels right. You like it; it catches your interest and seems to have possibilities; it makes you feel like writing more in the same vein. Your opening sentence has pleased you, the writer, and it is safe to go on.

10 STORY MIDDLES

Rhythm and pace

Just as well-written sentences and paragraphs have inbuilt rhythms, making the stresses fall where the writer wants them, good narrative too has its own rhythm. A book is put together section by section, and the larger rhythm is determined by the pace and length of these sections.

By pace I mean the rate of change within a piece of writing — the speed at which the story-section moves, together with the speed at which you feel compelled to read it. If all scenes are uniformly long and the pace is slow and reflective, with no development and nothing much happening, children's interest may flag. If scenes are uniformly short and the pace is very fast — brisk writing, with a lot of things happening in a short time — children may not have time to get their bearings in one scene before they are rushed off to the next.

When you are confident about story-telling, the manipulation of pace comes naturally; as Alinta climbs the stairs towards the cupboard where the unicorn is hiding, the story-teller's voice drops, time is stretched out, and pauses become longer (Slowly, slowly she climbed the first stair. Everything was quiet. She climbed the second stair . . .). At the climax the reverse happens: the story-teller's voice becomes louder, time is compressed and the pauses are shorter ('Got you!' said Alinta. She rushed at the unicorn, snatched the bag and ran downstairs again).

Your own ear is a good guide — try reading your story aloud to someone especially if you can put it aside for a couple of weeks first. If you suspect that your listener is counting the stripes on the cushions, or if you find yourself doing the same thing, poorly controlled pace could be the reason.

Watch out for scenes that occupy more than two pages, and ask why they are so long. Is it because a lot of information has to be conveyed? Or because the characters were busy talking and you didn't want to interrupt them?

Long scenes that have to convey a lot of information sometimes become unwieldly, and might be better broken into shorter ones. And when you finish your first draft and start revising, characters who talk too much will just have to be interrupted.

A story is defined by its forward movement. Characters can change their clothes, tidy their rooms, eat meals and quarrel with each other as much as you like, but if what they are doing in Chapters 1 and 2 has no bearing on what they are doing in Chapters 8 and 9, you may not be writing a story at all, but simply a collection of scenes. However interesting the scenes, if they don't add up to more than the sum of their parts, children — not to mention publishers' editors — will quickly become bored.

Foreshadowing

The story world is only a representation of the real world and doesn't necessarily correspond to it. In the real world certain events nearly always come upon us without warning: lottery wins and unforeseen accidents, though surprising, are no less believable than number seven buses. But if you try to bring them into a story as they occur in real life — that is, without warning or preparation — it doesn't work.

If you want proof of this, read a page (anywhere from Chapter 3 on) of any novel you like, finishing at the full stop closest to the end of the page. Now continue the story: take up the character you were reading about last and have them meet a sudden, untimely end in thirty words or less. You are allowed to use every artifice at your disposal to make these thirty words believable, but you are not allowed to change anything that went before.

Read the page again, and then read your continuation. Is it believable? My guess is that it is not. In spite of your vivid writing and your painstaking attention to truth and detail, the scene seems melodramatic and contrived, nothing like real life at all.

In this aspect at least the story world seems to work the opposite way from real life: in fiction, sudden events seldom occur suddenly — a space is prepared for them beforehand. In other words they are foreshadowed.

Part of the reason for foreshadowing is the satisfaction both writers and readers derive from the economical use of material — the same sort of 'coming home' satisfaction that you get from a Bach fugue or a Picasso painting. Beyond a certain point in the narrative, when all the necessary pieces and motifs have been laid down, a good story progresses and develops from within itself, using those same pieces and working variations on them.

An important event, such as the death of a major character, if it stands by itself and is unconnected to earlier events in the story, is dramatically unsatisfying; we expect a story to be shaped, and we expect there to be a place for all the events it contains.

Early screenwriters looked on foreshadowing with a sort of veneration. In old circus movies you can always pick which trapeze artist is going to die — it's the one who carries a rabbit's foot for luck. But foreshadowing doesn't have to be this obvious. You only need to allow dramatic events a space within the story and tie them firmly into the fabric.

For example, Luke's scholarship exam is a week away, and much depends on it. He is confident of succeeding, but to put his teacher's mind at rest he prepares carefully, even goes for a run on the beach the morning of the exam. He arrives at the examination hall fresh and in plenty of time, the order to start is given and he turns over the examination paper. And . . . What do you suppose? Does he answer every question and get top marks? Give yourself a few moments to think about it.

Of course he doesn't. After reading what I just told you, you already knew that. Would I have bothered to tell you all those details if I wasn't getting ready to surprise you?

Foreshadowing becomes even more important in stories where many hard-to-swallow events occur — in fantasy, for instance. (There's more about this in Chapter 11.)

Sticking to the point

In Chapter 6, I said that a story needs a point to aim at, some destination in the writer's mind. It's this destination that helps the narrator decide what to put in the story and what to leave out: the plot of *Little Red Riding Hood* definitely needs a wolf, but it can do without a swimming coach or an elephant or a pianist. The writer must stick to this aim and make sure that once the holiday destination has been chosen, we are not confused by pictures of other resorts.

This isn't always as straightforward as it sounds. If you have read this far you know how easy it is to construct imaginary worlds out of bits of your own experience. It's so easy that you can watch your unfolding story like a video; every detail of the setting, every movement, every nuance of colour and sound is clear to you. The trouble is that you may be tempted not just to write down every one of these details, which is fine, but to leave them in the finished draft, which may not be.

Inexperienced writers sometimes think they are supposed to write this way — that it's the writer's job to create detailed pictures, drag them into readers' heads and hang them there. The less adept the reader, so the belief goes, the more detailed the writer's pictures need to be.

In fact the opposite is true: the less skill the reader has, the more subtlety the writer needs — you need the ability to create characters, settings, moods, events and meanings out of the barest wisps of material, to avoid holding up the story. You can't transplant your vision into someone else's consciousness; what your readers see is their own picture, put together out of their own experiences, their own understanding of the words you use. Your job is to imagine the settings, characters and actions so that *you* believe in them, and then to reveal just enough to set off a parallel process in your readers.

More detail than you need will only pull the picture out of focus:

Annabelle opened the door and saw a tall man in dark glasses standing there. He was deeply suntanned, with black curly hair, and he was wearing a black silk shirt and sharply pressed fawn trousers. Round his thick neck he had a heavy gold chain, and he had a chunky gold bracelet on one hairy wrist, and a thin gold watch on the other. His hands were brown, with thick black hair on the backs, and on his little finger he wore a heavy gold ring with a ruby in it. He carried a black leather briefcase with a telephone in it; Annabelle could hear it ringing.

What do you think? The description gives us a lot of detail, but with all those details in the way it's hard to get a clear picture of the man who is being described. If you try playing round with different combinations of details, discarding the ones that are doing least, you will almost certainly end up with a description that is clearer, crisper and won't hold up the story.

Layers of meaning

So far I've tried not to talk too much about things like images, symbols and other pleasant surprises, simply because these things should find their way into your writing because you want them rather than because you think you ought to have them. But there is an important difference in the way that adults and children read, which affects the way good children's books are written — and that is where these pleasant surprises are important.

Adults seldom read a book more than once, but children under fourteen re-read their favourite books, going back to them again and again until they finally grow out of them. The fact that children read in this way gives writers for children a chance to do something special, and that is to write layered books. The outer layer is the slippery layer, in which you offer a quick and compulsively easy-to-read story that will force even reluctant readers to read on and find out what happens. Below that a good writer will include other layers to be explored on later readings, layers that contain subtle twists, variations, images, symbols, correspondences, analogies, insights, buried jokes and puzzles, or the author's views on life, the universe and nearly everything else.

Reading is more than a matter of decoding words, it's also a matter of knowing the conventions of fiction — the fact that an author doesn't waste a reader's time, or the fact that quests are always successful. Even though children's reading ability may vary — some will understand more conventions than others — their ability to recognise many of the subtleties of fiction is no less than that of adults. Children are at home with symbolism, for example, and use it in their own writing. They have to; for people whose skill with language is limited, symbolism is an important and expressive tool. They are also quick to read between the lines. In fact anything that children can do in their daily lives — and they are particularly good at reading people — they can do equally well in their reading.

The deeper layers you write into a story need to be delicately and subtly established, or they won't be layers at all, but just part of a crude upper surface; and this means writing in such a way that every word counts. If a story is cluttered with irrelevant images and descriptions, readers have no way of picking out the relevant one that is saying something.

It goes without saying that you can't have a multi-layered story without that slippery layer on top. Or rather, you can; but since few children would be able to read it you may as well not bother. If the upper layer of your story is strong, compelling and easy to read, children have a reason to read it a second, third and fourth time. And then they will find the plums and nice things you have hidden there for them.

Some things that go wrong

Even when you know where a story is headed, there are still ways of getting into trouble. A story can be boring; it can become distorted or run off the rails; narrative or characters can get stuck in one spot; you can get sick of the whole thing and either doubt your capacity to continue, or wish you had never started. Don't despair; with a little caution and commonsense, all these obstacles can be overcome.

Boring stories

To write a boring story is the greatest crime a writer for children can commit. It doesn't matter what else you do, but if your manuscript makes an editor want to put it down and do something interesting like washing up, you are in real trouble.

There are many ways to be boring, and I mentioned one of these in Chapter 1. Another is to be found among literate, linguistically talented but inexperienced writers. If you are guilty of this sin (and every writer has been guilty of it at one time or another) you may not be aware of it, and that compounds the problem.

In this sort of boring story it may look as if you have done everything right: story, characters and meaning may be beyond reproach; and above all, the language is literate. When you show the manuscript to family or friends they may not read it right through, but they are impressed. If pushed, they might hint that the story is just a fraction slow, but they won't admit they were bored by it — in the face of such literate writing, no one will own up to being a philistine. And so they tell you how well written your story is, and encourage you in your error.

The problem arises right at the beginning of the piece of writing, when you choose the narrator who is to tell the story. I talked earlier about auditioning narrators; you listen to opening sentences and finally pick the one that sounds and feels right. But if you are not completely at home with your material — if you feel nervous or inadequate, or less than passionate about what you are writing — you can make the mistake of choosing a 'writer' for the job. By this I mean that you choose a persona who is not really part of you, and who behaves the way you think a writer ought to behave — who says writerly things, and who talks at readers, instead of unfolding the story, so that at times we feel we are in a geography or history text book instead of in a story.

Stories can bore readers for plenty of other reasons, but those reasons are usually to do with the outer layers of a story — its execution. They are easily dealt with by either cutting or rewriting, and are covered in other parts of this book.

Distortion and the *deus ex machina*

As I've said many times before, a story is about a person. If during the course of a story about someone you change your mind and start telling it about someone else instead, the story is likely to be distorted and may even fall apart. Once you accept the idea that good children's stories are about people rather than things it's unlikely that you'd deliberately do this, but there is a more subtle way of usurping a central character's position. That is the *deus ex machina* in all its forms, 'the god out of the machine'.

The idea started in ancient Greece at a time when the demand for plays must have been particularly high and dramatists were having trouble keeping up; many a desperate *tragoidos*, on reaching the final scenes, would find the various conflicts so enmeshed there seemed no way of resolving them.

But instead of hurling themselves into the wine-dark sea, they found a more congenial solution. In the final scene an actor dressed as a god was lowered onto the stage by means of ropes and pulleys, and in the manner of Greek gods, rewarded those they favoured and punished those they didn't. The audience went home happy (or happier than they would have been otherwise) and the machine could be used again next time.

A *deus ex machina* is now the name for any last-minute plot intervention that has a similar effect: if it conveniently solves problems, is unrelated to anything else, draws undue attention to itself and gives the impression of clanking, it is probabaly a *deus ex machina*. Car accidents, sudden deaths (especially if you have more than one per story), fires, floods or earthquakes are all suspect if they occur near the end and conveniently solve more problems than they create.

A *deus ex machina* is frowned on in any kind of fiction, but there is one particularly troublesome kind that occurs only in children's books.

In children's fiction as well as any other, it's important that central characters solve their problems through their own qualities and their own efforts. Adults, being part of the real world, may need a place in its fictional representation — a story-world run entirely by children is seldom convincing — but when adults take over a story it quickly disintegrates. Look at these examples:

Janet and Alexander, mucking around near an old mine shaft, fall in. They are trapped there for several hours, calling for help, and try several ways of getting out but without success [So far so good. There is a story here.] until their parents hear their cries and rescue them. [And the story collapses.]

Melissa's father drinks too much, which causes her so much sorrow and embarrassment that she runs away from home. But then her father, overcome with guilt, has a change of heart and gives up alcohol and all ends happily.

Richard longs for a pet, and looks in every conceivable place for one. Then he has a birthday, and his parents give him a puppy.

Compare this last story idea with that of Philippa Pearce's classic, *A Dog So Small*, where the boy's wish for a dog is so strong that he apparently makes a dog come into existence.

Just how the problem in a story is solved is one of the most interesting parts. We want to see how characters work out their problem — not how someone else at the last moment works it out for them. This doesn't mean that friendly adult characters, such as teachers, can't give child characters a helping hand, but if they are not to be another kind of *deus ex machina* they should restrict themselves to helping.

Didactic stories

The problem of the *deus ex machina* partly explains why parents seldom play a large part in good children's stories — except, of course, in stories that concern a relationship with a parent. If the story is about some other, more private aspect of a child's life (and there are many) there might not be a role for the parents at all; and if there is nothing for the parents to do, a good writer will leave them out. In Philippa Pearce's *Tom's Midnight Garden* Tom stays with an old aunt and uncle who, not being used to children, never set foot in his world; in Lucy Boston's *Green Knowe* books all the children, for one reason or another, are separated from their parents, and are minded by an elderly lady who deliberately gives them their freedom.

Some adults who select or commission children's books are disturbed when parents are left out of the story like this; perhaps they remember poor quality fiction from their own childhood, and how parents were exiled to Africa or killed in car accidents so that something interesting could happen. Or perhaps they believe (as some do) that it is part of the writer's job to reflect the child's entire world, not just selected bits of it. It's a plausible enough view, until you realise that not only is any story necessarily selective, but that it's a short step from there to believing that writers for children have other obligations to adults: obligations to provide teaching material so that adults can teach children about sharing, animals of the world, honesty, co-operative behaviour, wearing seat belts, eating wholemeal bread and protecting the environment. Nothing wrong with that either? Maybe not. But what about stories that teach racism, competitiveness, aggression and chauvinism? They arise by the same mechanism.

Resist trying to use children's stories as a means of imposing an adult will, or of modifying their behaviour to make it more acceptable to us. The duties of a children's writer are to entertain and to enrich children's lives; there is nothing in the manual about having to be a police force. But while you are entertaining children, if you are writing honestly you will find that your own view of the world shines through all by itself, and that there is no need to force it down children's throats.

The never-ending narrative

When you read a good book for either children or adults you're not usually aware of any narrative structure. You are drawn into the story, and the fabric of it seems smooth and seamless, an unworked piece of real life. But an attempt to reproduce this seamless effect leads to a common mistake: the never-ending narrative, where the smooth, featureless writing just goes on and on, with no pauses or breaks, no shaping, and no distinction between important and unimportant events.

In a good book the narrative isn't usually as smooth as it looks — it's more likely to occur in a series of discrete lumps, with varying sized gaps in between. The gaps are the parts where nothing important happened — the places where the narrator knew it was better to keep quiet.

The act of story-telling in itself implies some selection, or you would start every story with the central character's conception, and every story would take a lifetime to read. (For a playful exposition of this and related ideas read Laurence Sterne's *The Life and Opinions of Tristram Shandy*.)

The problem is what to leave out, and this can become particularly troublesome at the ends of scenes. Sometimes a scene just trickles on and on, resisting all your efforts to move the characters to the next place. Even Laurence Sterne must have had this problem at times; Tristram Shandy sends out for a freelance critic to help him get his characters off the stairs, where they have been talking for several chapters, and into bed. The critic solves the problem for him by 'dropping a curtain' on the scene:

'— So then, friend! you have got my father and my uncle Toby off the stairs, and seen them to bed? — And how did you manage it? — You dropped a curtain at the stairs foot — I thought you had no other way for it — Here's a crown for your trouble.'

Dropping a curtain is as good a remedy as any. If you find characters at the end of a scene apparently stuck in the doorway, putting their hand on the door handle, turning it, opening the door, stepping through, and maybe chatting about inconsequential things at the same time, the best thing is to cut them off — finish the scene and start another one.

When your main character leaves a scene you don't have to follow them along the corridor, down in the lift, across the street and on into the next scene. Just cut to the next place and time where something important happens. Simple, ordinary expressions like 'a few weeks later', or 'when Alison got home' can be pure magic to stuck writers and their characters.

When a story feels wrong

I said that your feelings about what you are writing are among your most important tools, and I showed you how feelings can put you on the right track in the earliest, conceptual stages of writing. Feelings can also work in the later execution stages, letting you know when you have gone seriously wrong and need to turn back.

Unexpected journeys

Every writer knows it, that aura of doubt and dissatisfaction you get when a story has left the rails. There may be no fault with the actual writing — nothing you can put your finger on — but you can't shake the suspicion that you have gone wrong. At the end of the day you read what you have written and try to convince yourself that everything is still all right, but the irritable, depressed feeling persists.

However tempting it is to try, don't ignore the feeling. It usually means you know there is something wrong and are trying not to admit it. But this isn't the sort of problem that will go away by itself. On the contrary, if you don't deal with it now it will only get worse. Remember that as a writer you need to be responsive to your own feelings; if you get into the habit now of burying them and trampling on them, one day you may never find them again.

When the inner part of you knows that you have gone wrong, passion and conviction disappear. If your piece of writing is to progress, you have to get them back; which means that in this case at least, you must stop writing and look for the problem. As far as I know, there's only one way to find it. Go back to the point in your manuscript where this uncomfortable feeling began, and cut out everything you have written since then. (You don't have to throw it away.) If removing the material makes you feel as if a weight has been taken from your mind, good. Now you know what the problem was and you have fixed it.

If that wasn't the problem — if you don't feel any better, or if you couldn't find the exact spot where you went wrong — go for a walk, play some solitary sport or do some gardening. Problems buried deep within the story are then likely to surface, and once you know the problem the solution is only a step away.

Squeezing dry lemons

It's also possible you might just be having a bad day, though usually you don't have any doubts about that. On bad days nothing good happens at all; words won't form in your head, or if they do, they look silly when you write them down. You have an urge to throw out what you have written and write it again; but when you do write it again it doesn't seem any better.

This time the remedy is to keep on writing. No matter how little you produce or how slow and painful it is, on a bad day anything at all is better than nothing.

Strangely enough, the work you produce on bad days, once it is revised and polished, may not be very different from the work you produce at other times. This is why, when things aren't going well, you should resist the urge to keep scratching over what you have written. It won't work — half an hour later you will only want to change it again. Just leave it alone. Once you are sure you are more or less on the right track, keep going. If you absolutely must you can just fiddle with the words a little until your approximate meaning is clear to yourself, but then move on. Making the meaning clear to readers can come later on, when you are having a good day.

Brick walls

With the exception of some picture book texts, few pieces of writing go smoothly from start to finish. Stories seem to have built-in walls spaced along their length, just to make life hard for us.

The first wall lurks somewhere after the opening phase and before the halfway mark, and if you have not encountered it before you can be unpleasantly surprised. Just when you think everything is going well, and the story has started to develop and move by itself, you suddenly find you have doubts.

It's not that you can't think of anything to write — if you started with a goal you will already have some idea of that. It's more likely that you don't trust your ability to write it: the story is moving ahead under its own steam, taking you into unfamiliar territory, and all you have to guide you is the outline map you made. You may wish you hadn't started the journey at all.

This is the place where many stories curl up and die. You may not be able to avoid this wall, but you can prepare for it. If your story is based on your own experience you will have a passionate belief in it, so you won't give up easily. You will remind yourself that the good story you set out to tell yesterday is still a good story today, and worth seeing through to the end.

The existence of this first brick wall might explain why many writers like to keep an idea in their heads for weeks or even months before they start to write it down. During this time the story idea matures, collecting associations and peripheral ideas and gaining in depth. Not surprisingly, a writer feels a strong commitment to a story that has grown in this way. By the time it is ready to be written down — usually when the writer feels the idea has reached its peak and will soon start to decay — the writer's commitment is absolute, and no amount of difficulty is likely to make any difference.

Another wall can occur near the end of a book, when all the developments are over. You feel as if there is nothing left to discover; everything surprising or interesting has happened already, and now the downhill path seems predictable and boring. You wish for someone, anyone — editor, typist or good fairy — to come and tell you to stop work.

Unfortunately that last little downhill bit may run to three or four chapters when it's actually written down, and you are the only person who can do it. There is no writer anywhere who can write those chapters as well as you can — they are based on your own life and memories. Either you must do them yourself, or they won't get written at all.

The problem arises because if your story is going even modestly well you will always see further ahead than the scene you are writing. Eventually you will be able to see the path clear through to the end — no more obstacles, no more sudden turns or twists. And because you think there is nothing left to discover, the story as far as you are concerned is over.

But readers aren't mind readers, and so the tedious and (to you) obvious details still need to be written down. Before you can do that convincingly you have to believe in it yourself; you have to get back into the story and be part of it again.

One way of doing this is to look for a strong mood for the next scene before you start writing. You can try exploring the scene to see what interests you — what time of day is it, what sort of weather? How does your main character feel? How do the others feel? In a longer story you could try bringing in a new character you find interesting. This can be untidy in some earlier phases, but you can get away with it near the end, provided the character is a minor one and does not steal too much of the action.

Blank paper and blank mind
One morning you will sit down to continue a story you were working on yesterday, and find that your mind has gone blank. No matter how hard you try to pick up yesterday's work, nothing happens; you feel as if you are writing a sequel to the telephone book. It's all the more galling because

yesterday everything was going so well — the story was flowing onto the page all by itself.

In fact that's probably the reason for your difficulty today. If a piece of writing is going well you tend to keep writing, letting it all flow until the well has dried up. When there is nothing more to say the flow stops, usually at a natural cadence — the end of a section or chapter — and you tidy your desk and go to bed.

It's not surprising then that one day when you come back to work you will find the well is still empty, and no amount of clattering as you lower the buckets seems to help.

The easiest solution to this problem is not to let it happen in the first place. When you finish a day's work, leave something in your head for tomorrow. Avoid finishing at the end of a scene, chapter or section; if you feel you are getting tired and it will soon be time to stop, stop at a high point, where it will be easier to pick up the thread tomorrow. (If you don't trust yourself to remember it tomorrow, make a little note.)

If you can't resist coming back to the well just one more time, and it does dry up, the answer tomorrow is to keep writing. Don't try to continue what you were doing the night before — obviously that won't work — but jump ahead to another part of the story that you find interesting, and go on from there. Any part of the story will do. Don't worry about the gap you leave — you can easily fill it in later, when that particular well has filled up again. Relax! It will.

Writer's block
The child within you is not the only internal reader you have to worry about. There is often an adult reader sitting in there too, checking that what you write is good enough, even checking that what you write is suitable for children.

Sometimes this reader becomes officious and starts inspecting your thoughts even before you write them down, and this can cause trouble — you can freeze up until you can't write at all. Whether you have thought your story through or are just going to plunge straight in, a stern, critical reader is the last thing you want while you are writing. At such times William Cobbett's advice to writers is worth pinning to your wall, and in case you have forgotten it I mention it again: 'Sit down to write what you have thought, and not to think what you shall write.'

FANTASY

Strictly speaking, a fantasy is any story in which the rules of the real world are changed. A story in which animals speak, go to school or wear clothes is a fantasy. So is a story that contains impossible or non-existent characters (or highly improbable ones, depending on your point of view) such as dragons, bunyips, spirits, ghosts, or visitors from other worlds. So is any story that contains magic, and any story that is set in a different or future world.

Fantasies are probably no harder to write well than any other sort of story. Whether you are writing about the fiery desert of Tharg or a delicatessen in Brunswick Street the raw material comes from the same source, and the same principles apply. The same applies to fantasy characters; to the writer, a talking dragon may not be very different from the owner of the delicatessen, and is created by the same process.

But fantasy does offer a few difficulties of its own. Readers already believe in corner shops and the people who own them. In a story about the everyday world, as long as you don't reveal the machinery clanking underneath, all you have to do is keep the merry-go-round running and make sure no one falls off. But as E. M. Forster has pointed out, fantasy is a special ride. It demands a little more care.

Certain types of fantasy — stories in which a hard-to-swallow event takes place near the beginning — offer a particular difficulty. Even if you think you have got everything else right, the story is likely to come unstuck at the point where the fantasy begins:

> It was a quarter to four. Dust shimmered in the air outside the corner shop, and the dry smell of it mixed with the smell of hot chips and cooking oil. Hugo, who was standing in the doorway while he waited for the bus, found the smell irresistible, and searched through his pockets for a stray dollar coin. He was out of luck.
>
> But the smell of the chips was so overpowering that he found himself wishing more and more strongly. A moment later he felt a warm pressure on his palm and a gold coin appeared in his hand.

From that point on it's all downhill; no matter how hard we try, we can't believe in the appearance of that coin.

There seem to be only two ways of introducing an unbelievable event into a story: either suddenly, right at the beginning, in which case accepting the event becomes a condition for accepting the whole story; or gradually, later in the story. This way the ground is carefully prepared, and readers can get used to the idea a bit at a time.

If you add even one paragraph and a little extra detail to the last example, delaying the appearance of the coin, the passage becomes a little more believable:

> It was a quarter to four. Dust shimmered in the air outside the corner shop,
> and the dry smell of it mixed with the smell of hot chips and cooking oil.
> Hugo, who was standing in the doorway while he waited for the bus, found
> the smell irresistible, and searched through his pockets for a stray dollar coin.
> He was out of luck.
>
> There was no one to borrow from, either; when he looked along the
> footpath at the groups of boys in grey shorts and shirts he saw no one he knew
> well enough to ask.
>
> But the smell of the chips was so overpowering that he found himself
> wishing more and more strongly. It had to be possible. Anything you wanted
> this badly has to be possible. A moment later he felt a warm pressure on his
> palm and a gold coin appeared in his hand.

Even this slight slowing in pace has some effect.

You have seen the same thing in horror films. Trivial events like having a shower or washing up suddenly become important; the camera spends a long time looking at things we normally wouldn't be interested in, and instead of compressing days and weeks into minutes, now the camera stretches seconds into minutes instead. Can it really take so long to lock a door? To pull down a blind? And all the time we are on the edge of our seats, aware that something terrible is about to happen.

If a slow opening doesn't suit your story, you may prefer to take the other option and introduce the event right at the beginning:

> One afternoon as he was waiting for the bus, Hugo discovered he could
> materialise money.

This method has several advantages: it means you don't have to explain (unless you want to) how the coin got there, what it is doing there, or why the ordinary everyday world has suddenly become such a strange place.

Having produced your magic right at the beginning of the ride, you are free to start the merry-go-round.

This approach won't suit every story, or every writer. The story may demand that the magic enters later, and you may not be able to change that. In this case you simply go ahead with your story, placing signposts along the way reading 'This way to the magic'.

Fantastic events, even more than merely surprising ones, need careful foreshadowing. You can do it head on:

M. Louis Jean-Pierre Retif, head chef at The Jolly Swagman Barbecue and Grill, had always wanted a dragon.

Or you can be more oblique:

M. Retif always felt the cold in winter.

Or you can point in the opposite corner:

Louis did not believe in dragons.

Or you can tell us outright that something extraordinary is going to happen, but without revealing what:

If Louis had had the slightest inkling of what was going to happen to him that day he wouldn't have gone to school. He wouldn't even have left the house. He would have stayed in bed all day and told everyone he was sick.

Another important way of foreshadowing is to create an atmosphere that makes it easy for readers to believe that extraordinary events will follow. I am exaggerating, but you know the sort of thing:

Mandeville House stood high on a windy hill, its crumbling roof outlined against purple clouds . . .

What you do need to avoid is just marking time — telling us about everyone and letting them sit around and talk while we wait for the magic show to begin. Introducing extra plot lines will help to avoid this; you can introduce related situations that will point in the same direction as the main one, and thus give you an excuse to lay the necessary tracks. If you want to have a UFO take off from the back lawn one evening you might like to plan a fancy-dress barbecue for the same night.

When the magic does appear don't drop these related lines. Keep them in play at the back of your story, bringing them to the front every now and then to remind us they are still there, and then tie them off (or most of them) at the end of the story when you resolve everything else.

Paying attention to other aspects of the story is also a good way to keep it moving. Take care with rhythm and pace, and keep other motifs and parts of the plot — relationships between characters, for example — in motion. Allow characters to change their feelings about other characters if it seems appropriate, and plot the changes in relationships so that they take place gradually and credibly. Since this is essentially what stories are about, substrands about the characters (as long as these strands relate to the whole) will keep a reader's interest going even if there is no magic show at all.

A particularly tricky kind of fantasy story is the one where a fantasy character is to be a catalyst, entering the established lives and relationships of the other characters and changing them. At the end of the story it's usual for catalyst characters to go back where they came from, but this is a convention you don't have to observe.

It's also usual for catalysts to enter a story later rather than earlier, and this is a convention you might be stuck with; it takes time to set up the equilibrium that the character is going to upset. If you are writing about a family of four with a friend or two, that's a lot of equilibrium to set up, and if you are not careful the opening to the story can become quite slow and tedious.

Fantasy worlds

The construction and maintenance of fantasy worlds presents another set of problems. When people talk about fantasy this is usually the sort they mean — a story set in a dream world that is all the writer's own, created apparently out of nothing. To the uninitiated this is the aspect of fantasy that is so mysterious and so radiant; evidence of the human spirit at its most imaginative. It is also the kind of fantasy that wins prizes, perhaps for the same reason.

But to a writer, every setting, whether real-world or fantasy, is imaginative. It has to be; both sorts of worlds are put together out of exactly the same material. And far from being difficult or mysterious, a fantasy world may in some respects be easier to establish than a realistic one: the real world with all its institutions already exists, and a writer can't afford to get them wrong. But with a fantasy world no such limitation exists. If the author says a thing is so, readers have to accept it.

There are difficulties of course. One of these is the question of inner logic, or inner consistency — something that needs a good deal of concentration from the writer. The real world is directly observable. In the real world, if you can't remember the colour of the sea on a winter morning you only have to go and look. But fantasy worlds are not so easily checked. They are put together out of several imaginary jigsaw pieces, but that doesn't mean these pieces are going to form a logical, cohesive whole.

Ursula le Guin used to set an exercise that illustrated this point. The task was to create a setting by changing one aspect (only one) of the real world, and then to write a story set in it.

If you try the first half of the exercise — tracing the many changes that result from one change — you will see how much concentration it takes to keep the new world consistent. For example, what sort of world would we live in if the earth's rotation slowed to twenty-six hours; if everybody over twelve had a computer; if nobody had a computer; if humans had no sense of smell?

I ran up against this problem when I wrote about a family who lived in a house without electricity (*Message from Avalon*). It was hard not to forget and have them able to see things at night in rooms that were presumably lit with candles. (Fortunately, where I live there are frequent power failures, and so my memory was often refreshed.)

Lapses in the construction of a fantasy world — that is, lapses in the internal logic — are serious, since they erode the credibility not just of a situation or a scene, but of the story-world itself. One moment we look out of our chilly stone castle and see real trees, their bare branches lined with snow; the next moment they are made of polystyrene and cotton wool.

It might be because of this risk that beginners' fantasy stories tend to contain so much used furniture, bits and pieces of settings and ideas derived from other books in the same genre. Much of the furniture — magic rings and cloaks, mythical beasts and so on — is the legitimate stuff of fantasy. But there can be a problem; the European world in which these fantasies are often set contains among other things birch trees, fir trees, high mountains, icicles and blizzards, all of which may be unfamiliar to Australian writers. As we saw in Chapter 1, importing this sort of furniture in container loads from films and other books is not a solution. If you want the setting to feel real you will have to construct it yourself from your own experience. Have a winter holiday in Tasmania, or go walking in winter (with a bushwalking club!) in the Australian alps. Or create a totally different climate for your world, one that you have experience of and can believe in.

Sometimes the fantasy world is a future earth, and this produces its own difficulties. Ever since Sir Thomas More, writers have been trying to construct ideal worlds, and failing in the task. (It's an irreverent thought, but not even God was able to make an ideal world that contained independent characters and stayed ideal.)

This sort of world is not an easy choice for a story setting; by definition it contains no source of conflict, which reduces the story possibilities right from the start. This is why Utopia stories tend to look alike: the Utopians (the goodies) repel a threat to their ideal society from baddies who live outside it. Unfortunately, in this sort of story it's hard not to barrack for the baddies, who are so much more interesting, which undermines the story somewhat. (A refreshing change might be a Utopia which is destroyed by a goodie who is longing for Dionysian good times.)

There is also a pessimistic version of the future-world story — a dystopia — in which the world has succumbed to every form of misery the author can think of. Disease from chemicals and from radiation sickness is widespread, civilisation has disintegrated, and chaos is kept at bay only by an evil totalitarian Council. Again, there is a difficulty in maintaining the inner logic of this world; it's easy to remove electricity, gas, oil, telephones, industry, heating and even trees, only to find that you have given the Council sophisticated computer, surveillance and communications equipment with which to keep the society repressed.

Good fantasy worlds aren't created by chance. Like any other setting, a fantasy world comes together in a particular way because the author needs it that way. Finished stories are about people, but a new story usually coalesces round groups of ideas (including prefiguring ideas and settings) and emotional points: characters take shape round the emotional needs the author invents for them, and as the characters become established the author chooses the furniture for them — their families and friends and the places they will move about in. The difference with fantasy writers is that they are willing to consider more possible worlds, and more possible furniture for these worlds; and often the worlds come together before the characters do.

There is nothing wrong with this — you are allowed to put a story together in any way that suits you. But one thing you will have to watch is that you don't stumble into inconsistencies.

As we saw in Chapter 7 a useful device in any kind of fantasy is the first-person narrator. Because this narrator is also a character in the story we don't expect them to have a complete knowledge of the fantasy world, any more than we expect our next-door neighbour to have complete knowledge of the politics, economy, history, geography and ecology of our world. All either of them can see is their own corner — what they perceive themselves, what other characters tell them and what they can read about or deduce — and nothing else.

A first-person narrator brings additional benefits. As I mentioned in Chapter 7, merely telling a reader about an unfamiliar world can be boring. The best way for the reader to find out anything is through the action of the story. The least satisfactory way is when the author drops all pretence of story-telling and addresses the reader directly, with large slabs of encyclopaedia-style information.

You can get away with it right at the beginning, before the voice settles down and the story enters its first scene, but once we are into the story, we resent it if the narrator holds up a scene so as to deliver an explanatory lecture. A first-person narrator can get away with it; all by itself the first-person voice confers credibility — which is not the same thing as believ-ability; a first-person narrator can still dissemble. When the going gets tough, and the reader's credulity is strained, the first-person narrator can make a virtue of necessity by admitting it and saying:

> You'll never believe what happened next. If I hadn't been there and seen it with my own eyes I wouldn't have believed it myself. But . . .

But you won't get away with it more than once or twice. Any more than that and readers wake up to you.

Science fiction is also a branch of fantasy, but it's one you shouldn't attempt unless you have at least a little background in science — a degree, for example. If your background is shaky (only secondary maths, chemistry and physics) a kind person with an appropriate degree who is willing to stop you saying stupid things is also a big help. Science fiction worlds, too, have to be kept consistent; but here it is made more easy if you keep an eye on the laws of physics.

A common difficulty that arises when you write science fiction for children is that children know less science than you do (or you hope they do). This means that as well as telling the story you will somehow have to explain the science — and long passages of earnest lecturing will kill the story. One time-honoured way is to write in a character who knows nothing and has to have it all explained:

> 'Dr Schroedinger, what's this button for?' asked Henry, running his finger past a red switch on the right of the console.

Dr Schroedinger seized his wrist. 'Don't touch that! That's the automatic life support system flush.'

'That's too technical for me,' said Henry. 'You'll have to explain.'

And of course Dr Schroedinger does, for the benefit of the reader as well as Henry. But go easy on this device; remember that ignorant does not necessarily mean stupid.

One feature of fantasy stories that I haven't mentioned is language. For some reason richness of language takes on a new definition where fantasy is concerned, and I'm still not sure why. Language is a medium. Its job — in children's books at least — is to convey thoughts, ideas and emotions from the writer to the reader with as little distortion as possible.

But distortion must occur when the reader has no idea what the words mean. I'm not talking about a few unfamiliar words that are part of the narrator's speech, but about a whole narrative written in a foreign language:

> Potionmaster Dunk, espying the castle perched upon its hill with the green sward spread all about, desired the Runemaster to come to him and said 'Prithee, Lord Runemaster, do thou be quick and fetch me the fruit of yon pricklebush, that I might brew a Spell of Unseeing to keep our company from harm.'
>
> The Runemaster, who was a swart, stout man of good heart, did as he was bid . . .

You could perhaps make a case for this sort of language by pointing out that children need to be exposed to many different styles and vocabularies. True. The test is whether the archaic language actually helps the story. Sometimes it does; if the author is linguistically gifted, the language itself can be memorable, an essential part of the story's setting. If it doesn't — if the archaic language is merely clumsy and incomprehensible — you might be better off with language your readers can understand.

12 PICTURE BOOKS

Most of the unsolicited manuscripts that arrive on an editor's desk are stories for young children — that is, stories intended for picture books. In many picture books the text may be no more than a series of pegs to hang pictures on, and for this reason beginning writers are sometimes misled into thinking that these stories are easy to write. If they have a friend who likes to draw and has always wanted to illustrate, the mistake can be expensive: these apparently easy stories have the highest rejection rate of all.

Picture books come in two varieties — those written mainly by illustrators (and illustrated by them) and those written mainly by writers (and illustrated by illustrators). There are few if any books illustrated by writers.

First, the illustrator's book. It's rare for an artist to have equal expertise with both visual elements and words. If an illustrator conceives a picture book the idea is most likely to be a visual one, and the text may play a very small part indeed. Sometimes the text is so slight it barely exists except as a commentary on the pictures; it might state variations on a situation or idea, like 'circles', or 'big and little'; or it might report on an aspect of childhood such as 'bedtime' or 'in the park'. This is not to deny the value of this sort of text — some very beautiful and well-loved books fall into this category — but it's important to recognise that they are not usually written by writers.

The deceptive slightness of an illustrator's text often lures beginning writers into thinking they could do the same; and perhaps they could. If the text was all there was to it, just about any lively, imaginative person who understands young children could come up with a story that is no worse than many of the illustrators' texts that are published each year. But who would illustrate it? The illustrator is the front half of the donkey. The success of any picture book — whether it gets reviewed, how many copies it sells, how long it stays on the market — is in the first place determined by the way it looks. Books with very good pictures and indifferent texts sometimes even win prizes, but books with very good texts and indifferent pictures never do. A picture book, after all, is a *picture* book.

So the sort of illustrator who is able to breathe life into a shopping list is not likely to illustrate anyone else's shopping list, not when they can illustrate their own — unless, of course, the author of the shopping list happens to be someone famous or important.

The alternative you may be thinking of — giving your slight text to an artist friend to illustrate — is not a good idea. You may put your friend to a lot of needless effort and expense — artists' materials aren't cheap — and strain the friendship as well. What happens if the publisher doesn't like your text? Your friend will have worked for nothing. This is why picture-book texts by writers are usually submitted on their own.

Picture books written by writers also depend on the pictures for their initial success — most people who buy picture books choose them on the strength of the illustrations, no matter who has written the text. But this time there is a partnership, and both author and illustrator contribute special skills.

The writer's book, like the illustrator's, depends on a strong idea. Here the idea is less likely to be a purely visual one, and there will be more emphasis on form, language and meaning.

There is no room in a picture book to describe what the characters look like — there is scarcely a chance to 'draw' them at all, let alone flesh them out. This is the illustrator's job; but it's your job as the writer to provide the hidden matrix. A starting point can be a suggestive name, perhaps, or something important about the character: 'Mr Roseproud loved gardening'. But since that is about as far as you can go without cutting into words needed for the story, the illustrator will have to infer the rest of the characters from the text — from what they say and do.

To give the illustrator the best possible chance, you need to write a picture book with extraordinary care: to make sure that every single word you use is necessary, clear, accurate, the best choice, and in exactly the right place; that every single sentence is constructed in the most useful and most telling way, with the rhythms and stresses in exactly the right places. Then you painstakingly apply that fine-toothed comb to the entire text.

This kind of not-a-hair-out-of-place writing is satisfying, but not easy — you can spend hours trying to say something neatly in three beats when every way you can think of comes to six. Work on this scale demands it; revising and polishing a picture-book text is actually the same as writing it.

Whether the text is written by an artist or a writer, in the most successful picture books — those that last for more than ten years, for example — certain qualities seem to stand out: originality, impetus, warmth, structure, story, humour, honesty, point, credibility, elegance, and relevance to children. Don't slash your wrists if your story doesn't display all these qualities — I can't think of many that do — but it won't do you any harm to aim at as many as possible.

Originality

All picture books depend on a sound, original idea — an aspect of being human that hasn't been dealt with before, or a familiar aspect seen in a new light. This doesn't mean you should strive to be original; quite the opposite. Originality is something that comes all by itself when you are writing from within yourself, from your own feelings and perceptions. If you are writing from the outside — trying to impress readers with your originality — true originality will elude you.

It's not so much the bare idea that needs to be original as your way of treating it, and what you end up saying with it. Subjects like possessiveness, monsters, anger, holidays, isolation and fear of dogs have all been written about many times before, and they will be written about again; but successful books will have a point of view that is unique to their authors.

Impetus

There are certain fundamental aspects of a book — what it is and what it does — that affect how you write the story. Two of these are so obvious I hesitate to mention them, but I'm going to: one is that the pages of a book are intended to be read in a particular sequence; the other is that you can only see two pages at a time, so you have to make an effort — that is, turn the page — to see the next one. Compare this with a frieze, where you can see several pictures at once, and where you need to make no effort to see from one part of the frieze to another.

That is why a frieze doesn't need impetus and a book does; it needs something to force readers to make that effort and turn the page again and again. One way of achieving impetus is to have a strong, suspenseful story which draws a reader on to the reward of a resolution at the end; another is to offer a different kind of reward, perhaps a surprise, or a joke, each time the page is turned. Mem Fox's *Possum Magic* and Pat Hutchins's *Rosie's Walk* achieve their impetus through both kinds of reward.

If a picture book's impetus is allowed to slip — if the real tedium in the middle overshadows the imagined reward at the end — a child who is being read to is unlikely to complain. Being read to embraces a number of other pleasures, and needs no effort from the child. The problem shows when children are reading a story for themselves; they may still be happy to pick up the book and look at the pictures, but if impetus is absent or lacking, there is less chance the book will be read over and over again.

Warmth

In any good piece of writing, you expect the author to show the same human concern for their characters as a decent person would show for real-life people in the same situation. This doesn't mean that the narrator must withhold unpleasant details from us — far from it — but it does mean that we expect to sense a moral intelligence behind the words; we need to know that these details are part of what the author has to say, and are not there merely to satisfy the prurient.

In adult books, this is often the difference between literature and pornography, and the same sort of distinction can apply in children's books. In children's picture books the range of characters is wider, including not only people, but birds, animals, fish and insects. If in your story a child hits the cat with a stick, keeps a wild animal in a cage or sells his grandmother for medical experiments, we should know how you, the author, feel about it. I don't mean that you should shove the narrator aside and start preaching to us, but you should have an opinion. If your opinion is humane, sincerely held and goes beyond the merely obvious, your story will almost certainly have warmth.

Structure

A picture book can have any sort of structure at all as long as it makes readers want to go on reading. Structures that work take into account the fact that a picture book is a basic form, and the writer has to comply with it — not the other way round as with a novel. At the printer's the sheets of paper are folded in multiples of eight, yielding a book of thirty-two pages, or sometimes, if the publisher wants to make the book really cheap, twenty-four pages. (There are less common variations, but it's best to base your story on one of those alternatives.) By the time you have allowed for the half-title page (if you are having one), the title page, and space for publishing details, you may have only twenty-eight pages left for your story. Picture books are meant to be accessible to children who are just beginning to read. If you don't want to frighten them you will avoid putting large slabs of text on the page, and this means restricting yourself to around thirty words on each page, give or take a few. And that means your text should be somewhere between four hundred and two thousand words. If you have much less than four hundred your text may lack substance; any more than two thousand and you are moving out of the picture-book genre altogether.

It's not necessary for you to break your story into twenty-eight pages — you will have enough work to do writing it, and in any case the editor, illustrator and designer haven't made their contribution yet. But you should have some understanding of the form. For example, a picture book has built-in cadences — the small breaks that come between the left and right side of the double page, and the large breaks that come when you turn the page — and although you don't have to use these if you don't want to, you should at least be aware of their existence.

What I've said about structure in earlier chapters holds for picture books too, except that when you are writing on such a small scale structural flaws are magnified. If a novel or longer story is good in other ways, a disproportionately long opening may be no more than that; but in a picture book it may be a fatal disability.

The two basic story structures I told you about in Chapter 6 will work just as well for picture books, and the quest is one of the most popular forms of all. Perhaps its popularity comes from the fact that it seems so easy: a character has a problem, tries four or five ways of solving it, then discovers the right answer. There must be hundreds of successful books with this structure — and thousands of unsuccessful ones. Like longer quest stories, the picture-book version needs to have a goal of some consequence if you want children to read your book more than once.

Story

Although a picture-book text doesn't have to have a story (a text can take the form of a list, a report, a letter, a puzzle, or anything you like), in a writer's picture book the story is likely to be more important than it is in an illustrator's book. In fact I'll stick my neck right out and say that all long-lived picture books in which the text plays a large part contain either a strong story, or humour, or both. I can't think of one that has neither.

Good ideas for picture-book stories seem to be harder to come by than any other sort. Just about any personal idea you feel strongly about can start you off on a short story or novel; it is how you work it, how you develop the idea that counts. But a picture-book story doesn't give you that sort of freedom. There is no room for explanation, for developing characters, or for expanding ideas as you work. It all has to be contained in that one idea. You have to be able to hold a picture-book story in the palm of your hand.

It's true that the illustrator is going to fill in half the material, but that doesn't mean you can write your half and forget the rest. You still have to give the illustrator something to work on. The illustrator is guided by clues embedded in the text, but you have to put them there in the first place.

Part of the skill involved in writing a picture-book story is knowing what space to leave for the illustrator. This is sometimes interpreted as leaving out of the text anything that can be shown in the pictures ('red dress' or 'blue eyes') but there is more to it than that. Words can do much more than create pictures. A good writer uses them to their fullest extent, concentrating on what the words do best, and creating meaning through sound and ideas as an artist does through colour, form and line. Look at the difference between the Ahlbergs' 'Each peach, pear, plum', where the words lie so deliciously in the mouth, and its pedestrian précis 'all stone fruits'. And think of Hoban's Aunt Fidget Wonkham-Strong, who 'wore an iron hat and took no nonsense from anybody'; the words are not so much telling us what she looked like as what she *was* like — they are a thumbnail sketch for the illustrator.

The story in a picture book can work in much the same way as poetry, where sound, images, feeling and meaning can be so closely interwoven as to be inseparable. This is why a picture-book text doesn't have to seem sparse and empty without the pictures, as some editors have claimed. Though this is true of many illustrators' texts (especially those that rely on ironies between text and pictures), writers' texts on the whole tend to be more self-sufficient — normally I would expect a text of my own to stand on its own feet.

Slightness — where a story idea lacks substance — is probably one of the biggest problems with new writers' stories. (As we've seen, though, good illustrators are able to get away with it.) Its most common cause, I suspect, is writing a story too quickly. If you are writing a novel, the time it takes to write it down will often provide a sort of gestation period. But in a picture book, the inner and outer form must match so closely that the idea is just about all you get. If you write down a fresh idea without letting it brew first, it will lose its fluidity, and useful rewriting may be difficult, even impossible.

The other advantage of letting ideas lie in your mind for a while is that they sometimes overlap; where two ideas may not be enough for two independent stories, two or even three ideas together may well make one good one.

Picture-book ideas come from the same source as any other kind of fiction — from what you remember, feel and observe. Margaret Mahy has told how in an interview once, when she was asked where she got her ideas, all she needed to do was point; a dog had just walked into the nearby bank with a chequebook in his mouth. (But I suspect some people are lucky that way.)

You're not likely to find ideas for picture books (or any other kind of book) by going out and looking for them, but if you are in the right frame of mind ideas will come to you. An afternoon stroll past shops that say 'FAMILY BUTCHER' and 'FRIED . . . KEN' will yield more possibilities in a few minutes than an hour spent pondering at your desk.

These triggering ideas are all around you, but they work best if they are seen against a background of childhood memories. The childhood fear of being eaten seems to underlie Maurice Sendak's *Where the Wild Things Are*, and also strikes a chord with adults. (Who has not seen someone hug a small child and say 'I love you so much I could eat you'?)

Not all successful picture books have this adult appeal; some, like Raymond Briggs's *Fungus the Bogey Man*, have aroused adult revulsion instead. But the strength of this adult reaction suggests that Briggs simply found the other side of the coin.

H u m o u r

This is another essential ingredient, and together with story forms the heart of nearly all good picture books. In fact it's so important in its own right that it can sometimes replace story; humour can rescue a self-consciously poetic tract about Death or The Environment and let a child know that the world is not a place of unrelenting solemnity after all.

Humour can take many forms, but wit and general playfulness will always work better than a determined striving to be funny. Humour is like originality: if you had to try hard to get it you probably haven't got it after all.

One form of humour that works well in picture books is irony between text and pictures — where the words are saying one thing and the picture is deliberately saying another. Other forms you might like to consider are nonsense rhymes, exaggeration and playful repetition. Still another is the turning upside down of cherished adult ideals such as cleanliness or tidiness.

Honesty

There is one sense in which children's books, however fantastic, need to be honest. Authors shouldn't lie to children about the real world just because it makes a story easier to write — or possible to write at all. If you have in mind an unbearably sad story about a pet dog who is killed by a car you will have to decide whether the story is suitable for children, and whether you should write it. You can't make it suitable by saying at the end 'And then the dog came back to life again and everyone was happy'.

This is becoming more relevant as picture books enter another phase of their development. There was a time back in the 1940s and 1950s when lack of honesty was a problem with some picture books; aspects of the world that might disturb the idealised view of childhood were kept hidden, and one undistinguised book after another took its inspiration from elves, fairies and thatched cottages rather than from children's lives. (Though the Victorian preoccupation with sin and death meant that for a while death-bed scenes had been common in children's novels.) These days we are more inclined to believe that there is no topic that can't be presented in picture-book form. As the more obvious topics get used again and again (new baby, first day at school, visit to grandmother, fear of monsters) writers naturally search for topics that no one has tackled before. But the topics that are left are often the hard ones that no one else wanted — the very ones that it might be difficult or impossible to be honest about and still have an acceptable story. A story can lack honesty not just because of what it says, but because of what it doesn't say.

Point

The point is the inner reason for a story. The outward reason may be to make money, or to please a particular child, but buried inside the story should be its own reason for existing — something important it is saying to us.

Having something to say is not the same thing as moralising. There is such a thing as a moral point, but it is best made through the texture of the story, allowing readers to infer the meaning, rather than by direct preaching. Margaret Mahy's *A Lion in the Meadow* doesn't preach once, and yet the meaning is perfectly clear to us.

Whatever it is that a story is saying to us, it needs to be worth saying. No matter how strongly moral the point, if it's exactly the same point that has been made countless times before, or if it is so general as to be meaningless

('Don't do bad things, do good things') you may as well not make it.

The question of point in picture books is closely related to warmth. If you have a deep and personal commitment to what you are writing, if (to quote E. M. Forster again) you write with passion, you will write with warmth and also with something to say.

Credibility

Credibility in picture books doesn't mean you have to abandon all the bizarre, fantastic exaggerations that can make these stories so entertaining. It simply means that within the context of the story we should be able to believe what is happening.

Credibility means that we need to see the pieces of story-pattern fitting somewhere, and that we don't perceive them as disconnected, random events. This is obvious in stories about ordinary things like washing the dog, where a lack of pattern would make the story quite unreadable. But some inexperienced writers are misled into thinking that in fantasy all rules are suspended — that there is no more story-pattern, and fantasy events can take place at random, without causes and without effects.

Editors quite often complain that a story lacks credibility, and beginning writers almost as often complain that editors are wrong. But to help you make up your own mind, here is a question you can ask yourself: imagine the events of the story occurring in real life. Would you expect them to happen in this way, or is there a more probable way?

Here is another test. If you suspect your story lacks credibility, ask yourself honestly: do you believe it, really and truly, heart and soul? If you find yourself wriggling away and saying that well, this is for children, isn't it, and it's just the sort of thing they like, try again.

Elegance

I'm not proposing that picture books should glide around in silk and pearls, wrapped in co-ordinated laminated jackets, but elegance of a sort does apply to picture books. I am referring to that satisfying simplicity that is based on economy and accuracy. When you have only a few words in which to tell your story, they need to be exactly the right words, in exactly the right place and exactly the right order.

In a story, elegance is served by limiting the number of motifs you use. When you need extra elements, instead of bringing in completely new ones, you either work a pattern of repetition, or work variations on the motifs you have. In Russell Hoban's *How Tom Beat Captain Najork and his Hired Sportsmen*, the games played at the end are all variations on Tom's fooling around at the beginning.

Relevance to children

This seemed so obvious that I wasn't going to include it at all, but a glance at the correspondence following each year's Children's Book of the Year awards changed my mind.

It has been argued that picture books are for everyone, not just children, and that therefore there is a place for adult picture books — beautifully illustrated books with literary texts which somehow transcend the needs of mere children.

But adults already have their own literature. No matter what their reading taste, in the vast body of adult fiction there are more books than an adult could enjoy in several lifetimes, and more are being written every day.

Children's tastes in and attitudes to reading are still forming. What we give them to read now is likely to determine what they will be reading in ten or fifteen years' time — or whether they will be reading at all. Children's books should be important to all of us, but they are particularly important to children. Books help children to rehearse their adult personalities, and initiate children into our cultural life.

For these reasons I'm suspicious of those magnificently produced picture books with long, serious texts, which scratch exclusively adult itches concerning death, guilt, war, politics, whales or the environment. The exquisite, stylised pictures decorate these books without casting a single lumen of light on the text; and children are the losers. Children's resources are scarce enough without adults hijacking them.

Animal stories

These form a large proportion of published picture books, and an even larger proportion of unpublished ones. If you are thinking of writing animal stories there are one or two things you should know about them that will help improve your chances of success.

Animal stories tend to fall into two main kinds: those where the animal is mainly human, and those where the animal is mainly animal. There are some wonderful stories — such as Gene Zion's *Harry the Dirty Dog* — that straddle both kinds, but most fall into one group or the other. What you have to be careful of is writing an animal story that falls into neither. I'm not saying it won't work, but you do need to take care.

Furry people

Children already have an affinity with cute or familiar animals such as dogs, cats, mice, possums, koalas and rabbits, especially if the animal seems dependent in some way. It doesn't take much to turn an animal of this kind into a furry sort of person whom children will recognise and care about. *Possum Magic* is this sort of story; so are Russell and Lillian Hoban's *Frances* books.

The animals in furry people stories don't usually wear clothes these days, though they may occasionally live in houses and go to work or school just like humans do. Usually they live in families of their own species, but Jill Morris's *Dido has Diabetes* breaks with this tradition. Dido, a large and appealing diprotodon, lives with a human family and does everything that human children do except wear clothes. She talks, sleeps in a bed, has diabetes, goes to school, and has parties. The furry-animal aspect of Dido makes the idea of diabetes easier to accept — if Dido can accept it, we can — while the real life human background of the story — children, schools and hospitals — makes sure the problem isn't trivialised.

Furry people stories can be among the cutest of all picture books — few people can resist pictures of young furry animals — but if you are writing one of these stories take care *not* to be cute. Your characters still warrant respect. If they are animals you should allow them the dignity of being real animals, even when they are also people.

The affinity small children have with familiar or furry animals does not extend to creatures like ants, crabs, spiders, goannas, bees, snakes, mosquitoes, or even whales or dolphins, at least not yet. If you try to turn one of these into a person-animal you are likely to be in trouble from the start; without that affinity to build on, a picture book may not be long enough to let you construct the character properly. That may be why the books in which these less familiar animals are drawn as people often happen to be novels: Kenneth Grahame's Toad in *The Wind in the Willows*, Waldemar Bonsel's German classic *Die Biene Maja (Maja the Bee)* and E. B. White's *Charlotte's Web* come to mind.

But everything changes, and some animals that were familiar to children a generation ago (and therefore candidates for furry peoplehood) are no longer familiar except through soft toys and older picture books. Elephants, pigs, sheep, horses, cows and monkeys are gradually receding in favour of kangaroos, dinosaurs, wombats and possums; when children (and writers) become more familiar with dolphins, whales, emus, bilbies and echidnas we can expect them to join the list of acceptable animals. So even though when you were a child your favourite story was about an elephant who lost his red hat and muffler, think twice before you write a similar sort of furry-people story about a super-strong elephant who lives in a circus and forgets to do her homework. I'm not saying it won't work — anything's possible. But you would prefer it to work for a long time.

Animal animals

The other sort of animal story deals with animals as animals, and here you will find the less familiar or less appealing animals I have just mentioned. Animals in these stories may have one or two human attributes to help bring the point home, but in essence they are animals, not people. Unless their lives have been affected by humans, they live in their own habitat, eat their natural food, don't wear clothes or watch TV, and are less likely to talk. Thelma Catterwell's *Sebastian Lives in a Hat* falls into this category.

In the more successful stories of this kind the author chooses a topic that is relevant to humans as well as to the animal, and this increases our involvement in the story. Because both humans and animals at times share the struggle for survival, this is a common subject in books of this kind.

Inanimate objects

Inanimate objects don't seem to work as characters in picture books. There are few successful picture books about a stone, shell, tree, cloud, or building; it would take a great deal of skill and many words to turn something with no remotely human features into a character we can believe in and care about. Patricia Wrightson did it in her novel *The Nargun and the Stars*, but it's unlikely you could perform this trick in a mere thousand words; and it's asking too much to expect an illustrator to do it for you. Drawing a funny face on a rock isn't enough.

But as inanimate objects approach the human they acquire possibilities. Clothing and soft toys, for example, even trains, are easier to turn into characters than clouds, brooms or power tools.

After taking up most of this chapter to tell you what you ought to be doing, I should also tell you about a successful book that fits none of the preferred categories: Jean Chapman's *The Terrible Wild Grey Hairy Thing* (illustrated by Vicky Kitanov), about a sausage that rolls into a corner of the kitchen and metamorphoses into something unspeakable, is one of the most entertaining picture books I know. As I said right at the beginning of this book, there are no rules.

13 REVISION AND AFTER

Revision

One of the big differences between beginning writers and experienced ones is that experienced writers are better at seeing the flaws in their work before they send it away. Once you can see the flaws you have some chance of putting them right, but beginners typically have trouble seeing them. All the steam seems to go into that first heady puff of creation, and there is nothing left for what most writers would think of as the real business of writing: the painstaking evaluation, cutting, shaping, revising and polishing that defines a finished piece of work.

It's part of a writer's apprenticeship to learn what a good piece of writing looks like, and to make sure that their idea of it coincides with that of editors. But if you have just spent several exhausting months writing a manuscript, now that it's finished you will feel more like partying than picking holes in it. The last thing you want is to go through your manuscript again — after all, you might find something wrong with it. And so you are tempted to send the work out as it is — beautifully typed, maybe even bound in a special folder, but essentially unrevised.

You might as well send pages from the telephone book. It is axiomatic: unless your story is very short indeed, and you have carefully polished it as you worked, your manuscript will need revision. All manuscripts do. Things change even as you write; characters by the time you get to the end might be incompatible with the way you have drawn them at the beginning. You will have become a better writer by the time you get to the end, and the early chapters may be dull and clumsy compared with the way you write now. Or the whole piece, while essentially there, may be diffuse and hard to get into.

This thought horrifies some writers. But my guess is that if you started off using your own material you will have an investment in your writing, and you won't want to abandon it until you have communicated your feelings to your readers. For this reason, to many experienced writers revision is the most enjoyable part of writing. The risk and excitement of discovery may be over, but now there is the quiet satisfaction of shaping and polishing until the piece of writing says what you want it to.

At the first draft stage, writing is often at its best when it just happens; when, like Alice, you don't know what you think till you've said it. If you are relaxed when you write, words, images and situations that have meaning for you will keep recurring in one variation after another. Eventually they will form their own pattern of correspondences and repetitions, and reveal the meanings that you set out to find.

Or almost. This is the first draft, and when you read through it, here and there you will see motifs and ideas that are unclear, or that seem to contradict the meanings that are emerging. You may see the meaning, but the chances are it's still veiled by layers of potch. Revision is what lets you polish it and turn it into something sparkling and precise.

If you have no idea where to start revising, put the manuscript away for a few weeks. When you get it out again, even if it still looks fine, put it through the typewriter one more time. Typing it out yourself seems to work better than making corrections with a pencil and getting someone else to type it; paradoxically, entering the story again yourself as author–reader helps you to find roughnesses you might miss as author–editor. Even without conscious effort from you, retyping will usually sharpen the story — writers are naturally lazy, and have a tendency to save work by cutting anything that isn't essential.

Sometimes the faults in your writing hide from you. The desire to write something excellent is overshadowed by the even greater desire to have already written it. Even if you know the piece is not quite right — reading the story gives you a vague, dissatisfied feeling instead of the warm glow you had hoped for — the exact faults may stay obstinately hidden.

But as we've seen, that feeling of vague dissatisfaction with your work is valuable, almost as valuable as the ability to see the faults clearly. Never ignore it. New writers tend to see their work through an optimistic haze, so any sense that things aren't quite right is worth cultivating. If you can't find any big faults to put right, start working on the little ones. Faults are magnified when someone else sees them; what you see as harmless little bumps, and hope no one else will notice, will actually look like plague buboes to an editor.

Making the best of rejections

Even if you give your story a thorough overhaul before you send it, if it is one of your first half dozen attempts it might still come back to you. Rejections as well as revisions are part of your apprenticeship.

A bulky envelope addressed to you in your own handwriting doesn't have to ruin your day. The publishers are not sending it back to you because they hate you, or because they think you are a lazy, untalented no-good person who probably drinks on the side. It's simply because they didn't think your manuscript would make money for them.

The thing you want to know is why. If you can find that out, you will have a better chance next time. Unfortunately it's hard to get editors to reveal what their idea of 'good' is — or even 'bad' for that matter.

Rejection letters seldom contain any clues. In case you haven't seen one before, they look something like this:

> Dear Ms Brainchild,
>
> Thank you for sending us your story, *The Peppermint Loan*. Unfortunately our lists are full and we are unable to accept it. However we wish you well with it.

Or from very gentle or very squeamish editors:

> We very much enjoyed reading your story, *The Peppermint Loan*. Unfortunately it is unsuitable for our purposes and we are therefore returning it.

A letter like this can be misleading, sometimes giving a desperate writer false hope when they should be looking at the manuscript to see where it went wrong. A rejection like this is still a rejection. It means that for one or more reasons, your manuscript was not what the publisher wanted. You can react in several ways. You can go to bed with a huge block of chocolate and not talk to anyone for days; you can stuff the parcel into the bottom of the wardrobe and never write again; you can send it straight out to another publisher; or you can finish the chocolate, look at the story again, and try to work out why it came back. If you do manage to find the reason, you need never make that mistake again.

The editor who does the rejecting is the person best placed to say why, but unfortunately all a rejection letter usually does is express the editor's regret. It will seldom say why she regretted, or even if she regretted regretting. And it doesn't tell you if you're on the right track — if this story was better than the last one, or how close you came to success. It even ignores the wistful little request you enclosed with your manuscript: 'If this story is not suitable I would very much appreciate your critical comments.'

Most editors don't have time to give comments on rejected manuscripts. They are too busy earning their salaries, working on the manuscripts they didn't reject.

For writers, it's a frustrating time. We all remember it — the time when we were desperate for some authority to tell us what we were doing wrong. Writers in this condition turn to their own children, other people's children, writers groups, parents, friends, spouses, established writers, schoolteachers, librarians, booksellers, neighbours — anyone at all who once read a book or thought about reading one — in an attempt to get the information they need.

But you are the only person who knows the answer. You are the one person in the world who knows precisely what feelings of gentle regret, calmness, rage or sorrow you were trying to convey. If you give your story to other people to read, and your intention doesn't emerge from the writing, what sort of advice can they give you? None that is worth having, unless they are clairvoyant.

Once you grasp that truth — that you are the only expert on your work — another one follows: there are no such things as Editing Elves. Every writer at one time believes in the shadowy Elves who live in drawers and under desks in publishers' and printers' establishments. Their sole function is to correct the little things — those details that are so tedious for an author to follow up: inconsistencies (like a Vegemite sandwich on page nine that becomes a peanut-butter sandwich on page twenty); misspellings; grammatical uncertainties; words that are nearly right, but not exact; lumps and clumsiness in the writing; a dénouement that is too boring to write out in full; a scene that nearly works but that comes unravelled in the middle. The Elves use either an attachment screwed onto the typesetting machine, or — in more traditional establishments — a sprinkling of magic dust.

There is a stage in every piece of writing when an author wants to call in the Editing Elves; when you know what work still needs to be done, but can't bear the thought of the hard labour that goes with it. It's tempting then to imagine that all this menial work you are shirking should really be done by an editor. Experienced writers know the warning signs, sigh, make a cup of coffee and keep on working. But beginners who believe in the Elves often finish their manuscripts at that point, and you know what happens then.

If your spouse or children or friends haven't come up with the sort of answer you were hoping for, the following list might help. It's a list, not in any particular order, of the most common reasons for rejection.

Wrong choice of publisher

If your story has possibilities but still isn't quite right, not all editors will see those possibilities. It may depend on a publisher's house look — the genre within a genre that a particular editor creates over time. If your book doesn't fit this look, its possibilities may remain unrecognised, by this publisher at any rate.

This is particularly true if your story is intended to be a picture book. Not all children's editors have expertise with picture books. Not all will have access to exactly the right illustrator for it; and not all are good at visualising from a bare text. If an editor can't see your book in her mind's eye — if she can't get some idea of the kind of book it would make — she will reject the story. (In case you are thinking of helping out by including an essay about the story, don't.)

It's possible for a story to travel round to many different publishers and be rejected by each of them, until one day an editor sees that all it needs is a change or two . . . and *presto!* A best-seller. But it's rare.

Wrong sort of publisher

Another reason for rejection is that you have chosen a publisher who doesn't publish children's books — something that can happen if your only source of publishers' names is the phone book. Publishers of tertiary text books don't publish children's stories. Neither may those who specialise in cookbooks, atlases, or books on house and garden improvements. But since some do, you will need to check. The easiest way is to go through the Australian children's book section at your bookshop — ask the bookseller first as a courtesy — and take note of the names and addresses of those publishers who are producing books similar to the one you have written. A copy of the current *Writers and Artists Yearbook* will also help.

The story wasn't the editor's cup of tea

Even if your story is well written and entertaining, and has something to say to a wide range of readers, and even if you have chosen the right sort of publisher, it doesn't mean that this publisher will accept it. An editor just might not like it; it might remind her of the problems she is having with one of her own children at the time, or she might be coming down with the flu. Believe it or not, it happens. Editors love to regale one another with stories of big ones that got away (from other editors, of course).

Something was seriously wrong with the story

I have to say it: this one is the most common. But if you suspect that this is the reason your story has come back, there's no need to be depressed. The quality of the story is the one variable you have complete control over. By eliminating poor quality as a reason for rejection you are guaranteeing yourself success.

Now that you have come this far you will have a good idea of what constitutes quality in children's books, but to sum up I can repeat this advice: use your own childhood experience; remember that good stories are about people; and make every word count.

What makes a writer's apprenticeship harder than most is that novice writers aren't sure what they are supposed to be producing. Editors can't tell them, for fear of limiting their choices, and they can be specific only when they are telling you what they don't want. Essentially, what all editors are looking for from new writers is something new as well as good. That means a completely new voice and a new way of looking at things: something as unique to the writer as fingerprints or genetic code.

The best way to get a feeling for what is wanted is to read a variety of children's books — a thing that aspiring writers don't always think of doing. From libraries you can find out what children's books have been doing in the past, what they are doing now, and what they are likely to be doing two or three years from now. It can take months for a new book to appear in libraries, so a bookshop may be a better bet; if you have a friendly bookseller you might be able to make a deal: offer to buy new titles and return them in a day or so, in pristine condition, for a 90 per cent refund. This is a reasonable suggestion only with picture books — novels you will have to buy in the usual way. But if you buy a lot your bookseller may give you a discount. Try to read at least some books soon after they appear. One of the most valuable things you get from reading recently published books is a sense of current trends.

Beginning writers who don't do their homework sometimes lose touch with current trends; nervous of swimming in unknown waters, they find themselves falling back on the stories they knew in their childhood. Every editor has seen countless rewrites of *The Magic Pudding*, *The Gumnut Babies* and *Emil and the Detectives*, not to mention rewrites of stories that were bad in the first place — rewrites of hundreds of stories about fairies, gum trees, kookaburras and thatched cottages that were churned out in the 1940s.

About age groups

There is one more thing you should know before you start your next book: how to make sure you don't write the wrong one. This question doesn't arise when you are writing for adults; you just start writing, and it turns out to be itself and stands or falls on its own merits. If you write an excellent adult novel that is outside the usual length for books of its kind, you can expect that its excellence will eventually win through and someone will publish it. With children's books this is less likely to happen; the idea of excellence includes suitability for a market niche. For a picture book the idea of 'excellence' includes the requirement that the story will fit into 24 or 32 or 36 pages, leave room for the pictures, and be accessible to children under ten.

Good writers who are in touch with their inner child know about market niches, but they know it in their bones. They don't deliberately set out to write for an age group; instead, story ideas fall into existing niches apparently all by themselves.

In fact some good writers — and their publishers — have claimed there is no such thing as age groups, and that the lists put out by night-school writing classes (the ones that set out age groups with related information) are so much hogwash. Age groups, they say, are nothing but a construct, an artifice that enables publishers to define their markets.

Whether or not you believe that age groups exist, it's not a bad idea to aim at straddling them. As we saw before, children read differently from adults; where adults read a book only once, children read favourite books over and over again, coming back to them at different ages. If the books are good ones, children will find something new in them each time.

But even if age groups are irrelevant, the market niches that they are based on are not. Spanning age groups is a good thing; missing them entirely is not. Here is a list of the market niches that currently exist for children's fiction. It's a good idea to know them; few publishers would risk stepping completely outside them — and certainly not with an unknown author.

Picture books

These are books that have at least half their content in illustrations, nearly always full colour. Picture books are usually thought of as being suitable for children from two to ten, and although that's something you could argue about, it's better not to be too noisy until you have had one published. The length of a picture-book text is usually 32 pages (occasionally 36 or 24) and the text varies from no words at all to around 2000. The Children's Book Council's Picture Book of the Year is drawn from this category.

Picture story books

These have rather more text and rather less illustration than the previous category. The story is more complex and detailed, and the colour illustrations may be interspersed with line drawings. The length ranges from 1500 to 5000 words. Perhaps because these books, which are in the picture-book tradition, tend to be beautifully produced, the Children's Book of the Year for Younger Readers is most often drawn from this category.

Junior novels and short-story collections

These are intended for children between seven and ten who want a longer, more grown-up story — which is why publishers design these books to look like adult paperbacks. Humour seems to be an essential ingredient. The length ranges from 5000 to 10 000 words, and the books are often illustrated with line drawings. I am not sure why — whether judges are put off by the humour or the cheaper production — but The Children's Book of the Year for Younger Readers is not often drawn from this category. As far as I know, there is no reason it shouldn't be.

Novels and short-story collections for children between nine and fourteen

The length varies from 20 000 to 50 000 words, and because these books are intended for more adept readers, there are no illustrations. Some publishers have complained that this niche, like the one before it, has been harder to fill; either writers are less interested in it or there is less encouragement for it. The Children's Book of the Year for Older Readers is occasionally drawn from this category.

Novels for young adults

I have mixed feelings about these, and don't believe a book on writing for children is an appropriate place to discuss them; after all, they are intended for young *adults*. But since The Children's Book Council's Children's Book of the Year for Older Readers is most often drawn from this category (defined by the Council as 'books which require mature reading ability') I have included it here for the sake of completeness.

In these novels the central character is around seventeen, and the story, as you would expect, is told against a background of concerns of seventeen-year-olds — getting a car, doing exams, going to university, getting a job. Some splendid novels have been written in this category — and also a good many duds. The length varies from about 40 000 to 85 000 words.

Presentation

The way you present your manuscript can tell an editor all sorts of things, not only about the story but about you. If your presentation differs too much from the standard, it can affect the frame of mind in which an editor reads your work. If it comes down to a borderline judgment, a sloppy or pompous presentation might just tip the scales against you; a simple, unassuming but professional presentation might tip the scales in your favour.

A handwritten manuscript can tell an editor that the author is either a child or not a serious writer. Most editors won't read handwritten manuscripts at all; some, very occasionally, will read a handwritten picture book text provided it is neat.

Amateurish typing can also damage your chances, giving an editor the impression that you don't know what you're doing. You're supposed to be a writer — a person whose business is words. Use a machine on which all letters work, and which neither skips spaces nor puts them in. Check that your spelling and punctuation are accurate, and make sure you leave one letter space after each punctuation mark. Don't use flimsy, discoloured, creased or dog-eared paper.

A manuscript that has started to yellow with age or has coffee rings on it tells an editor that this manuscript was refused by all the more important publishers it was sent to, and that the author doesn't have enough faith in it even to bother retyping it.

You don't have to have a sloppy presentation to put an editor offside. An over-grand presentation will do it too. It's not a good idea to have your manuscript professionally typeset, even if you can do it on your boss's computer. Forget about trying to make it look like a real book, and (unless of course you are an artist) forget about illustrations. Publishers like to think that they are doing the publishing.

Even if you are an artist, it's best to get the text and roughs approved before you do the final illustrations. The editor might want a tiny change in the text — such as turning 'dog' into 'cat' — and the whole book will have to be rejected.

Type your manuscript on one side only of good quality A4 paper, using a newish ribbon (very new ribbons are sometimes over-inked, and the result looks messy). Set wide margins all round (4–5 cm is OK), use double or one and a half spacing between lines, and number the pages where the editor can see them easily — top or bottom right or centre are all suitable. Identify each page with a header or footer giving a short form of the story's title together with a short form of your name; if the editor takes manuscripts to bed with her, you don't want bits of yours getting mixed up with someone else's.

Finally, type a page showing the story's title, your name, your address and phone number, and maybe the number of words in the story. At this point most beginners like to add some strong clip or binding to their manuscript, in the fear perhaps that their story will end up as paper aeroplanes in the editor's office. For very short texts some sort of fastening is fine, but have you ever tried to read a longer manuscript that was fastened with non-removable clips? Worse, have you ever tried to read one in bed? The manuscript snaps shut at the clip, and you have to wedge it with a pillow; or the pages pivot on the clip and tear out, and there's no way to get them back in again. If you want to make the editor interested in your work, make it easy to read. Don't fasten it at all. Just send it off in a close-fitting box with a lid, and enclose a short friendly covering note.

The covering note is the first sample of your writing that the editor is going to see, and it's worth taking a little trouble over. If that first letter comes across as stilted, distant or bossy, what will that say about the rest of your writing?

Be kind to the editor: keep the note short. It can be either handwritten or typed, as long as it's on a large sheet of unlined paper (small scraps of flimsy paper look mean, and have a way of disappearing). Write the note in your own voice. Don't lapse into letterese just because you have something pointed in your hand; no herewiths or please find encloseds — just a friendly 'here is'. If you can come up with a brief, cheerful, spontaneous comment, one that will reveal you as a warm, entertaining, thoughtful and intelligent human being who is obviously going to write many best-sellers, put it in by all means. You might like to finish by expressing the hope that the editor likes the story, but no more than that.

Many new writers, having got everything else right, finally lapse into mortal sin at this point. If your story is newly finished and you feel good about it, you may be tempted to start sharing it with the editor at once, even before she has read it. And before you know it you are writing a covering letter that tells all about your story — why you think it's good, where you got the idea, why you wrote it, and what colour socks you were wearing at the time.

In the future

Whether we like it or not, our society thinks of children as lesser beings — not just smaller than we are but less important; and everything to do with them is thought to be less important too. There were laws protecting adults from underweight bread centuries before there were laws protecting children from dyes such as copper arsenite in their sweets; laws protecting adults against watered beer long before there were laws protecting children from flammable nightwear. At the time of writing, laws in Queensland prohibiting prostitution still don't protect children from procurement for prostitution, and the possession of child pornography has only just been outlawed.

This long-held attitude to children and their world forms a background to all our dealings with them, and so it shouldn't surprise us to find that children's literature too is considered less important than its adult counterpart. In every weekend newspaper you can read reviews of adult fiction; children's books, despite forming over 30 per cent of the total market, get less than 1 per cent of the review space.

Even people who are dedicated to the cause occasionally slip up. How many children's writers have said at one time or another that they weren't really *children's* writers — that they actually wrote for themselves? (Redfaced, I raise my hand.) But how many teachers or librarians have said proudly 'Sarah is such a wonderful reader! Only nine years old, and already she's reading *The Thorn Birds*!'

Somewhere the misconception has crept in that children are really an inferior sort of adult, to be judged according to how well they fit in with the adult world. In the adult world, the most rewarding literature is often the most difficult to read — I think of Trakl's 'barbed wire against the uninitiated' — and at the other extreme, the easiest reading is often the least rewarding.

This Golden Ladder view of literature, in which children's picture books are seen to occupy the bottom rung of the ladder, with junior novels on the next rung, novels for young adults further up, and the nirvana of adult literature at the top, seems to be gaining ground. Subtly, it is invading all our opinions on children's books; now, if we come across a children's book and it's funny and also easy to read we relegate it to the lowest section of the ladder without even looking for literary merit. And if we come across a book that is boring, cruel, humourless or frigid, as long as it is difficult to read, and as long as the main character is over fifteen, we hold it up like an icon. This book, we say, is *challenging*, and therefore good for children. But a book doesn't have to be hard and boring to stretch young readers' minds. It can also contain layers of meaning, as I've suggested in Chapter 10.

To see children's literature in this way is to ignore what good children's writers have been trying to do for the past hundred years: to bring a literature to children that is within the range of their abilities, but which sacrifices nothing in the way of literary content.

To make things worse, we haven't yet shaken off a Calvinist attitude, which says that if children's books are fun, they can't possibly be any good; and if in spite of everyone's efforts entertaining books exist, a proper didactic use had better be found for them. Most children's books in Victorian times were intended to warn, inform and improve the mind and moral fibre. How many children's books these days are selected 'because they teach how people live in other lands' or 'because they teach about safety' rather than because they are literature and fun? This is the only reason I can think of for the fact that the work of Paul Jennings has been so consistently ignored by the children's literature establishment.

Writers — and not only children's writers — have good reason to be worried. In the first place, the Golden Ladder view of literature adds weight to the idea that children's books are disposable: that they are not only easy and trivial, but not worth keeping in the shops for more than a couple of months. The other reason is that although younger children are nearly always keen readers, when children get to between ten and fourteen many of them start to lose interest. Some escape and become non-readers altogether. If writers of adult fiction are to survive, the writers of children's fiction must find ways of holding on to readers. What better way to do this than to provide them with books that they like? Books they can actually read, that have interesting stories, that will stick to their ribs and offer something for later. In other words, good books.

I hope you will write some.

BIBLIOGRAPHY

The following is not a list of Approved Books and Authors; many of my favourites are not included. It is simply a list of books that are mentioned in the text (see page reference), or illustrate a point, or that you will find interesting in some way.

Adams, Douglas, *The Hitch Hikers' Guide to the Galaxy*, Pan Books, 1979, (p. 32)

Boston, L. M., *The Children of Green Knowe*, Faber & Faber, 1954, Puffin, 1975, (pp. 22, 49–50)

Briggs, Raymond, *Fungus the Bogey Man*, Hamish Hamilton, 1977, Picture Puffin, 1990, (p. 92)

Calvino, Italo, *If on a Winter's Night a Traveller*, Picador, 1982, (p. 37)

Catterwell, Thelma, *Sebastian Lives in a Hat*, illus. Kerry Argent, Omnibus, 1985, Puffin, 1989, (p. 97)

Chapman, Jean, *The Terrible Wild Grey Hairy Thing*, illus. Vicky Kitanov, Ashton Scholastic, 1986, (p. 97)

Disher, Garry, *Writing Fiction*, Penguin, 1990,

Fox, Mem, *Possum Magic*, illus. Julie Vivas, Omnibus, 1983; 1991, (pp. 40, 88, 96)

Grahame, Kenneth, *The Wind in the Willows*, Methuen, 1931, Puffin, 1983, (p. 96)

Greene, Graham, *The Power and the Glory*, Heinemann, 1940, Penguin, 1969, (p. 25)

Hoban, Russell, *How Tom Beat Captain Najork and his Hired Sportsmen*, illus. Quentin Blake, Cape, 1974, Piper Books, 1988, (pp. 40, 95)

—— *The Mouse and his Child*, illus. Lillian Hoban, Faber, 1969, Heinemann, 1985, (p. 40)

Hutchins, Pat, *Rosie's Walk*, Macmillan, 1968, Picture Puffin, 1970, (pp. 27, 88)

Jansson, Tove, *Moominpappa at Sea*, Puffin, 1974, (p. 25)

Kästner, Erich, *Emil and the Detectives*, Jonathon Cape, 1959, Puffin, 1971, (p. 104)

Krauth, Caron and Nigel, *I Thought You Kissed With Your Lips*, Penguin, 1990, (p. 49)

Lindsay, Norman, *The Magic Pudding*, Angus and Robertson, 1918; 1983, (p. 103)

Mahy, Margaret, *A Lion in the Meadow*, Dent, 1976; 1986, (p. 93)

Morris, Jill, *Dido has Diabetes*, Greater Glider Productions, 1992, (p. 96)

Nesbit, Edith, *The Story of the Treasure Seekers*, Puffin, 1958, Purnell, 1983, (p. 40)

Pearce, Phillipa, *A Dog So Small*, Penguin, 1964, Puffin, 1970, (p. 72)

—— *Tom's Midnight Garden*, Oxford University Press, 1958; 1989, (p. 72)

Rice, Scott (comp), *It was a Dark and Stormy Night*, Penguin, 1984, (p. 64)

Sendak, Maurice, *Where the Wild Things Are*, Bodley Head, 1967, Picture Puffin, 1970, (p. 92)

Sterne, Laurence, *The Life and Opinions of Tristram Shandy*, Houghton Mifflin, 1965, OUP, 1983, (p. 73)

White, E. B., *Charlotte's Web*, illus. Garth Williams, Hamish Hamilton, 1952, Puffin, 1969, (p. 96)

Wrightson, Patricia, *The Nargun and the Stars*, Century Hutchinson, 1973, Puffin, 1977, (p. 97)

Zion, Gene, *Harry the Dirty Dog*, illus. Margaret Bloy Graham, Bodley Head, 1960, Picture Puffin, 1970, (p. 95)

INDEX

accents, 58
Adams, Douglas, 32
adjectives, 10
adverbs, 55
age groups, 104–6
Ahlberg, Allan and Janet, 91
Auden, W. H., 7

Bonsel, Waldemar, 96
Boston, L. M., 22, 49, 72
Briggs, Raymond, 92

Calvino, Italo, 37
Catterwell, Thelma, 97
Chapman, Jean, 97
characters, 18–25
  and memories, 8
  and self, 18–19, 25
  and sentimentality, 25
  animal, 95–7
  believability of, 18
  changing flat to round, 20
  creating, 18–21
  describing, 21–3
  flat, 20
  gender of, 24
  'good' or 'bad', 25
  inanimate objects as, 97
  influence of TV on, 23–4
  naming, 18–19
  round, 20
  setting as, 25
Chekhov, Anton, 56
childhood, using memories of,
  5–9 passim, 11
Cinderella, 44–5, 48, 51, 57
Cobbett, William, 26, 63, 77
condescension, 29
conflict, 12
credibility, 94

de la Mare, Walter, 19
deux ex machina, 70–2
dialogue, 52–8
  and accents, 58
  and attribution, 52–4

doing more than one job,
  55–6
  starting a story with, 61
Dickens, Charles, 22
didacticism, 72

elegance, 94
emotion, 12, 15, 16, 37
emotional significance, 11
editors, 101–2
experience, 5–12 passim, 14,
  16–17

fantasy, 47, 78–85
folk stories, 40, 46
foreshadowing, 66–7, 80
Forster, E. M., 12, 78, 94
Fox, Mem, 40, 88
frigidity, 12

Gardner, John, 12
Garfield, Leon, 14
gender, of main characters, 24
Grahame, Kenneth, 96
Greene, Graham, 25

Hoban, Russell, 40, 91, 95, 96
honesty, 93
humour, 92
Hutchins, Pat, 27, 88

ideas, 6–9, 91–2
  and originality, 8, 88
  combining, 16
  for picture books, 88, 91–2
  from other books, 7
  prefiguring, 6–7
illustrations, 27, 86–7, 91
imagery, 31–2, 68–9
imagination, 12, 13, 16
impetus, 88
intensity, 10
irony, 91, 92

Jansson, Tove, 25
Jennings, Paul, 109

Kitanov, Vicky, 97
Krauth, Caron and Nigel, 49

landscape, 25
language, 34–9
  and rules, 34, 38
  dictionaries and style manuals,
    37–8
  in fantasy, 85
  rendering accents with, 58
  sexism in, 33, 35–6
  use of ordinary, everyday,
    34–5, 39
le Guin, Ursula, 82
Little Red Riding Hood, 24, 67

Mahy, Margaret, 92, 93
meaning,
  layers of 68–9
  of experience, memory or
    story, 6, 16, 17
  writing to discover, 6
memory, 5–12 passim, 14, 16
mirror, 23
Morris, Jill, 96

names of characters, 18–19
  in dialogue, 52–4
narrative,
  first person, 47–9, 83–4
  neverending, 73
  second person, 49
  third person, 49–51, 60
narrative, viewpoint,
  limited, 47–51
  objective, 45–6, 60, 63
  omniscient, 46–7
narrator, 23, 44–51, 60, 70
  role of, 64
  voice of, 62
Nesbit, Edith, 40
notes, making, 9, 42

observations, 7, 18
originality, 88